WINNER OF THE PAUL A. BARAN – PAUL M. SWEEZY
MEMORIAL AWARD

Established in 2014, this award honors the contributions of the founders of the *Monthly Review* tradition: Paul M. Sweezy, Paul A. Baran, and Harry Magdoff. It supports the publication in English of distinguished monographs focused on the political economy of imperialism. It also applies to writings previously unpublished in English, and includes translations of new work first published in languages other than English. Please visit monthlyreview.org for complete details of the award.

PAST RECIPIENTS

*Imperialism in the Twenty-first Century:*
*Globalization, Super-Exploitation, and Capitalism's Final Crisis*
John Smith

*The Age of Monopoly Capital:*
*Selected Correspondence of Paul A. Baran and Paul M. Sweezy, 1949–1964*
Edited and annotated by Nicholas Baran and John Bellamy Foster

*Value Chains: The New Economic Imperialism*
Intan Suwandi

*Capital and Imperialism: Theory, History, and the Present*
Utsa Patnaik and Prabhat Patnaik

## Praise for *The Dialectics of Dependency*

"In these times of monsters, summoned by a moribund capitalism, in these times of deepening inequalities across the continents, Ruy Mauro Marini returns to us in this book with his stiletto-sharp Marxist analysis of dependency. Having read this book, having debated its theories, you are obliged to go out there and advance the cause of humanity."—Vijay Prashad, Tricontinental: Institute for Social Research

"Ruy Mauro Marini (1932–97) was probably the most important founder of Marxist dependency theory. It is therefore all the more curious that his most important essay, *The Dialectics of Dependency,* was published in many languages, but never in English. Amanda Latimer, backed by Jaime Osorio, has now changed that. Not only has she translated the key text, but she also added an excellent essay on Marini's intellectual biography, while Osorio's essay introduces readers to the debates surrounding underdevelopment and revolution in Latin America of which Marini was a part. May this book be widely studied!"—Marcel van der Linden, International Institute of Social History, Amsterdam

"*The Dialectics of Dependency* is a classic work of Latin American social thought and an inspiration, even if its author, Ruy Mauro Marini, did not intend to produce a text with this end in mind. It is a text that is linked to a life of struggle and political formation inside and outside of the academy. Almost fifty years after its appearance, the book's theoretical, methodological, and political force calls for both a careful re-reading and for boldness in efforts to update it, in response to the dilemmas of our times. Ultimately, inequality will either be overcome by socialist revolution or will tend to intensify labor super-exploitation, whether in the center or the periphery. . . . With the present translation, the English-speaking reader has in his or her hands an important key to explaining the inseparable relationship between imperialism and dependency. Welcome to the battle of ideas inherent to the fertile struggles of the 1960s and 70s in Latin America!"—Roberta Traspadini, Professor in International Relations, Federal University for Latin American Integration (UNILA), Brazil

"With his essay, *The Dialectics of Dependency*, Ruy Mauro Marini offered Marxist theory a new key to aid in its task of explaining a world built by capital. The subordinated regions and economies of the world system have the theoretical tools to account for their subordination—for the obstacles to growth and the welfare of their population, the reasons for starvation wages, and for the poverty that affects the majority of wage earners. The peoples of Latin America, Africa and Asia can themselves explain the reasons for their persistent rebellion: the fruits of their backbreaking labor feed local businessmen but also the bourgeoisies of the world centers of power and wealth, in so far as the capitalist world economy favors the transfer of surplus value. As local capital and imperial capital form an alliance of planetary plunder, so too do the struggles of the paupers of the dependent world and the peoples of the imperial nations demand mutual nourishment."—Jaime Osorio, Chilean social scientist in exile and former colleague of Marini, Mexico

"Translations are the first step towards building broad but unified anti-imperialist struggles in Asia, Africa, Latin America and elsewhere. At long last we have an English translation of Ruy Mauro Marini's seminal work *The Dialectics of Dependency*, contextualized brilliantly by Amanda Latimer and aided by Jamie Osorio's 'Notes on the Dialectics of Dependency.' As they navigate this book, which has been informed by a spirit of internationalism, readers may wish to ask: Had the text been translated five decades ago, how might it have changed the course of debate on dependency, imperialism and neo-colonialism throughout the Third World? A must-read for Marxists and non-Marxists alike."—Radha D'Souza, Professor of Law, University of Westminster, UK

"Readers have had to wait for almost half a century for the publication in English of this groundbreaking text by the Brazilian social scientist Ruy Mauro Marini, revealing the North's disregard for social scientists, particularly Marxists, from the South. I do not exaggerate when I say that this book has the potential to profoundly change our understanding of the South's dialectical process of dependency on the North and of the capitalist development of the world system."—Cristóbal Kay, Emeritus Professor, International Institute of Social Studies, Erasmus University Rotterdam

"Those of us focused on issues of development such as dependency and underdevelopment welcome this long overdue translation of Ruy Mauro Marini's important theoretical contribution of a half-century ago. Its significance is enhanced by Amanda Latimer's translation to English and deep historical contextualization and synthesis of Marini's life, thought, and influence with past and present progressive movements. Jaime Osorio contributes an insightful prologue on the relevance of the Marxist theory of dependency and a postscript on capitalist development and the super-exploitation of labor."—Ronald H. Chilcote, Professor Emeritus, University of California, Riverside, and Managing Editor, *Latin American Perspectives*

"*The Dialectics of Dependency* has become a classic of Latin American social thought because it addresses essential issues with an original approach and with a resonance that time has only confirmed."—Emir Sader, coordinator, *Encyclopedia Latinoamericana*, and author, *Lula y la izquierda del siglo XXI*, Brazil

"*The Dialectics of Dependency* is a compelling contribution to the enduring struggle against imperialism over the past 500 years of capitalist development. Ruy Mauro Marini's seminal work has advanced our knowledge of class struggle under conditions of super-exploitation and the imperialist forces which subjugate the global South. Amanda Latimer and Jaime Osorio bring Marini's powerfully influential book to English readers. An essential book for understanding imperialism."—Immanuel Ness, City University of New York

# THE DIALECTICS
# *of* DEPENDENCY

## Ruy Mauro Marini

*edited by* Amanda Latimer and Jaime Osorio

*translated by* Amanda Latimer

MONTHLY REVIEW PRESS

*New York*

Editorial material © 2022 by Monthly Review Press
Translation © 2022 by Amanda Latimer
"Dialectics, Super-exploitation, and Dependency: Notes on
'The Dialectics of Dependency'" first appeared in *Social Justice*,
volume 42, number 1. Used with permission.

Library of Congress Cataloging-in-Publication Data
available from the publisher.

ISBN paper: 978-1-58367-982-1
ISBN cloth: 978-1-58367-983-8


Typeset in Bulmer MT Std

MONTHLY REVIEW PRESS, NEW YORK
monthlyreview.org

5 4 3 2 1

# Contents

# Prologue: The Relevance of the Marxist Theory of Dependency

JAIME OSORIO

How important for the English-speaking reader is the current edition of Ruy Mauro Marini's "The Dialectics of Dependency," a work originally published some fifty years ago in Spanish? Does this book have any relevance for our times?

A little history will allow us to situate in broad strokes the emergence of the issues that the Marxist theory of dependency and "The Dialectics of Dependency"—the main work in this theoretical project—sought to explain, and the new horizon that Latin American Marxism opened up for the world's peoples.

More than five hundred years ago, European kingdoms such as the Spanish and Portuguese initiated a period known as the "Age of Discovery," lasting until at least the nineteenth century. Maritime expeditions were encouraged and financed with a view to locating new trade routes. These expeditions traveled around the globe and encountered new lands, peoples, and cultures for the Europeans, leading to their conquest and domination. This spurred an increase in commercial exchanges and the advance of mercantile capitalism.

In this context, a Genovese navigator named Christopher Columbus, at the command of three vessels and after a voyage that took two months and nine days, arrived at a small island in the Bahamas called Guanahaní. It was an exploratory voyage sponsored and partly financed by the Spanish Crown, aimed at discovering a new route to reach the Indies through the Atlantic Ocean. The motivation for the search was that the known route to Asia passed through the Mediterranean Sea, which was under North African control. Thus, in a somewhat fortuitous fashion, on October 12, 1492, Columbus reached what would later be called the Americas.

The Portuguese Crown also set out in search of new routes to the Indies. Vasco da Gama, on a long voyage in 1497, traveled along the coast of Africa and reached Asia through the Cape of Good Hope. In 1499, Amerigo Vespucci, a Florentine merchant supported by the king of Portugal, crossed the Atlantic and reached Brazil's northern coast, then sailed in a southward direction. This is how the reconnaissance of Brazil took place, after having been initiated by the Portuguese Pedro Álvarez Cabral, the first of the European navigators to reach those lands.

Vespucci's initial voyage was not particularly successful in terms of discovering precious metals. However, it allowed him to understand that the lands he had reached were not the West Indies, as even Columbus initially thought, but rather a new continent. In honor of this realization, in 1507, the German cartographer Martin Waldseemüller named the new continent "America."

But the search for new routes to the Indies was also motivated by a desire to increase the procurement, and reduce the cost, of spices such as cinnamon, ginger, and pepper. These were considered the "gold of the Indies," products that fetched high prices when traded in Europe and yielding significant profits.

It is quite correct to say that, from the end of the fifteenth century onward, the foundations were laid for history to be approached as truly universal history. After the encounter with the Americas, an entire, enormous continent and its riches (which had been ignored by the learned, the churches, and the European and Asian kingdoms of the time) was now integrated into the economic and political processes fostering a nascent capitalism, to which it would give a powerful impulse.


With the aim of obtaining more knowledge of these new lands and their riches, the frequency of voyages to America began to increase. The Iberian kingdoms, later joined by England and France, encouraged these expeditions. Columbus himself made three additional voyages over a period of ten years, reaching the coast of Central America in one of them.

Following these voyages, and with the direct testimony of explorers who spoke of abundant precious metals and a wealth of animal and plant species in the New World, the Spanish kingdom began preparations to send massive contingents of people. These included officials, soldiers, small merchants, and numerous clergymen, all ready to conquer the new lands and evangelize Indigenous people.

Thus began the conquest and the subsequent period of colonization, from the sixteenth to nineteenth centuries, of the territories of what has been known primarily, since the second half of the nineteenth century, as Latin America.

It was advisors to the expansionist French empire in the nineteenth century, under Napoleon III, who promoted the use of the term "Latin" in this context. Their aim was to open the region to greater French presence and break the monopolies enforced by Spain and Portugal. Using the presence of peoples speaking Romance languages (Spanish, Portuguese, and French) as justification, they chose to refer to "Latin" America rather than "Hispanic" America, as it had been called by the Spanish Crown. With the collaboration of local writers and thinkers, there would soon be a consensus about the French formula.

The conquistadors and colonizers established territorial divisions, authorities, laws, and regulations to maintain their rule over local cultures and peoples. Many of these peoples already had advanced knowledge of construction (attested to by the ruins of Machu Picchu, a city for the ruling caste of the Incas, priests and military, located in Cuzco, Peru, and by the pre-Hispanic pyramids in various parts of

Mexico) and of astronomy (as demonstrated by the Aztec calendar). Among many other achievements, they developed methods of irrigation and the construction of aqueducts (also evident in Cuzco), civil engineering projects on bodies of water (the city of Tenochtitlan, in Mexico), horticulture, writing, trepanation, fine pottery works, metalwork, weaving, and embroidery.

To encourage expeditions, the European kingdoms offered titles of nobility and land to expedition leaders. The conquistadors, and later the colonial authorities and founders of towns and cities, were charged with locating deposits of precious metals, accelerating their exploitation, and facilitating their transfer to the Iberian Peninsula.

The ships carrying this gold and silver were of great interest to pirates and corsairs—these were initially French, later joined by the English and Dutch—which led to their frequent sinking following naval skirmishes. The losses were not minor ones. For example, between 1587 and 1592, English pirates captured more than 15 percent of the silver destined for Seville. Most of these spoils went to royal funds, but some went to banking and commerce. The pillage was such that the British Crown knighted many pirates as payment for their services, Sir Walter Raleigh and Sir Francis Drake being two of the most notorious cases.

Over the course of three centuries, the conquistadores and colonizers' zeal in increasing shipments, which came to include raw materials and many kinds of food, caused the death of untold thousands of Indigenous people due to the long and exhausting workdays to which they were subjected. Further, the invaders brought heretofore unknown bacteria and viruses, against which the Indigenous population had no defenses, leading to numerous deaths from disease. This reduced and exhausted the available workforce. It is estimated that, by 1492, there were some 65 million Indigenous people in what is now Latin America, mostly concentrated in Peru and Mexico. By 1700, less than two centuries later, this figure would drop to 5 million. According to experts, it is one of the largest genocides known in modern times.

This spurred a search for new sources of labor, which would ultimately be solved by enslaving and shipping millions of people from

Africa to Latin America. Between 1525 and 1866, some 11 million enslaved Africans were transported to the region from diverse parts of Sub-Saharan Africa (mostly from what are today Angola, Senegal, Congo, Guinea, and Cabo Verde). This population was not constituted by migrants, but by enslaved people, whom *negreros* (slave traders) transported to the New World's ports under royal charter. Many Africans were simply kidnapped in the interior and then bought by Europeans on the coast. Sometimes the companies established for this trade (e.g., the Royal African Company) acquired them from local traders in exchange for rum, cigarettes, and weapons.

More than 36,000 direct transatlantic voyages took place in this three-century time frame. The licenses for these voyages yielded significant revenues for the kingdoms of Spain, Portugal, and England, as well as Holland and France, where the main shipping companies and merchants that undertook these voyages were headquartered. Brazil was by far the main recipient of enslaved people in the world, reaching a figure of 6 million. After Brazil, came the English, Dutch, French, and Spanish holdings in the Caribbean. Mexico, Central America, Colombia, Peru, and Ecuador also received significant numbers of enslaved people, but many fewer than Brazil.

The African, Indigenous, and European populations comprised the main groups that, in varying proportions, populated the colonies and then the nation-states of Latin America. Later, Asian, Arab, and new generations of European immigrants would arrive. This generated a great cultural mosaic, expressed in diverse culinary and musical traditions, beliefs, clothing, color palettes and aesthetics, rituals, legends, and literature.

By the beginning of the nineteenth century, there was a considerable presence of several generations of the colonizers' descendants. Having been born in the region, they were called "Creoles" to differentiate them from the Spanish. Many worked in areas related to production and commerce, which brought them into prolonged conflict with the colonial authorities. This was due in part to the trade monopoly that

the Spanish and Portuguese monarchies exercised over the purchase of
the colonies' products.

These conflicts became intense at the beginning of the century, when
Napoleon Bonaparte's troops invaded the Iberian Peninsula, forcing
the abdication of King Ferdinand VII of Spain. After a period in which
Napoleon's brother, Joseph Bonaparte, was crowned king, Ferdinand
would return to the throne in 1813.

This was the time when, in most Latin American colonies, independence movements took the initiative, beginning the process of
rupture with the colonial empire. In most cases, it was Creoles at the
head of companies or leaders steeped in the new political doctrines
from France and England who led these efforts. The English supported many of these independence movements, since by doing so
they opened up a vast region for the expansion of their commercial
and productive capital.

Since the European empires "discovered" Latin America, its history
has been closely intertwined with the rise of European capitalism, and
with the ongoing shaping of what would become the capitalist world
system. At the core of this system are the relations between capitals
of different regions. These become connected in such a way that the
shared processes have repercussions in each region, but with very different consequences.

The extraction of precious metals from Latin America to Europe
played a fundamental role in fostering Europe's nascent mercantile
capitalism and in the accumulation of capital that would later make
viable England's Industrial Revolution.

Between 1503 and 1660, an estimated 185,000 kilograms of gold
and 17 million kilograms of silver entered the Spanish kingdom from
its New World colonies. Since it took another 150 years for these colonies to become independent, in the nineteenth century, the final figure
should be understood to be much higher.

Apart from the intense pillaging by pirates, Latin American gold and
silver destined for Spain had other routes which took it to England and

various European regions. Since Spain failed to develop manufacturing and industrial activities by that time, such products were mainly acquired from English and French companies. These were enormous purchases, because they had to cover the needs of the peninsula's population, as well as those of authorities, civil servants, military personnel and their families in the numerous New World colonies. Furthermore, the Spanish Crown undertook multiple military and defense operations in Europe between the fifteenth and nineteenth centuries, which entailed substantial expenditures in equipment, transport, armaments, and food for troops. To maintain the Spanish kingdom's war machine, Charles V and Philip II had to incur debt, issuing bonds to Genovese and German bankers. All of this led to high levels of debt and interest payments. Coins minted in Spain—from silver that was mostly obtained from the mines of Potosí and Zacatecas—circulated in Central and Southern Europe as international money; rarely were they put to productive ends. Due to their high value, these coins were highly sought after in the ports and cities of India and China, where they tended to be hoarded, as well as sought by the merchants and money-lenders of Europe.

After independence, the former Latin American colonies pivoted to European markets, particularly England, which was eager for foodstuffs to feed its growing urban and salaried population, and for raw materials to supply its revolutionary industry. In this context, one of the central tasks was meeting the requirements of capital reproduction then taking shape in the spheres of production and circulation. All the while, there were efforts to unite the territories with shared political projects—following not infrequent civil wars—and to form nation-states.

Shifting from a world of colonies to one of formally independent states brought considerable changes for Latin America. Dependency, or the subordination of economies and states to other economies and states, began to take shape, which entailed a departure from the colonial condition. This process would assume differentiated and nuanced characteristics over the course of its historical development, but it always favored the emergence of semi-colonial economies and regions.

At the same time, the transition implied the birth of a local process of capital reproduction under the command of local ruling classes. This process would adapt over time, driven by the shifts undergone by and requirements of imperialist capitals at the heart of the capitalist world system, and of the international division of labor then taking shape.

During the colonial phase, payment of tribute, taxes, tithes, as well as pillage and plunder, were key to generating surpluses that were mostly appropriated by the Spanish Crown and local ruling classes. However, after independence and with the further maturing of capitalism and the world market, it would instead be unequal exchange, accompanied by profits on investments and interest on debt payments, that constituted the primary mechanisms by which imperialist capitals benefited from the transfer and appropriation of value.

The development of some regions and economies, and the under-development of others, are the simultaneous but divergent results of the forming of the capitalist world system and of the relations established among regions. None of these processes, on the whole, can be explained by considering regions and economies in isolation.

In England, initially, technological advances made it possible to raise production and flood local markets with a growing mass of commodities. Although a part of this production was exported to other regions and economies, such outlets were limited, so the expansion of the domestic market was mostly achieved by actively incorporating workers into consumption. This was an essential step in the effort to complete the cycle of reproduction.

The supply of food from Latin America made it increasingly possible for English capitalism to reduce the value of labor power and thus achieve a balance between increasing surplus value and, at the same time, increasing wages. This in turn favored a mode of capital reproduction that had to maintain a significant connection with the capacity of the wage-earning population to consume. It was a link that could be loosened, but not completely broken.

By contrast, super-exploitation—that is, the remuneration of labor power below its value—became the fundamental mechanism that local capitals in Latin America used to supply foreign markets with raw materials and foodstuffs, and to become competitive. The fact that Latin American capitalism did not have to generate an internal market, as long as English, other European, and U.S. demand absorbed its product, is key to explaining the weight of super-exploitation in the reproduction of dependent capitalism from the very beginning. In dependent capitalism, the dominant classes were (and still are) more concerned with the consumption of workers in the imperialist economies to which they sell, than that of the local working population.

For this reason, unequal exchange between imperialist and Latin American capitals gained momentum, and super-exploitation in turn became the key mechanism used to compensate for the resulting loss of value. However, that form of exploitation also curbs the productivist drive that is supposedly inherent to all capitalism. In a dependent economy, that drive is inverted, leading to intensified exploitation, reinforcing the tendency whereby the local workers' consumption does not constitute a significant market for regional capitalists. Even with better wages, workers will not demand copper, lithium, iron, or wood pulp (which is what they produce). By contrast, they will turn to eating bananas, avocados, and tomatoes, even if not the better-quality ones that are exported or which find their way to high-end local markets. Even less, in our time, can they acquire cell phones, new or used automobiles, or television sets because the "neoliberal pandemic" of the twentieth and twenty-first centuries, and the Covid-19 pandemic of the latter, have driven down their already miserable wages.

Super-exploitation, in turn, is possible because Latin America's productive apparatus is limited so that labor is abundant and new workers are always available to replace those prematurely worn out by excessive working hours and poor nutrition.

It is one thing to form export economies such as that of Germany or present-day South Korea, where the capacity to compete in the world market rests on the upgrading of the technological and productive apparatus. It is quite another to create economies such as those of Latin America, whose capacity to export and compete in the world market rests mainly on low wages and the extraction of raw materials. This generates very distinctive forms of capitalist reproduction.

The bourgeoisie and landowners in dependent economies are mainly responsible for ensuring that this situation persists and is reproduced. As long as this arrangement permits them to appropriate substantial profits, partly through converting a portion of the workers' consumption fund into a fund for capital, these classes have neither the will nor the political disposition to change the prevailing order.

The dominant classes' responsibility in reproducing dependency—which does not imply discounting the role of imperialist capital—is one of the political conclusions of the Marxist theory of dependency. This position separates the theory from all previous and current critiques of contemporary capitalism, which continue to assign a role to local ruling classes in essentially utopian projects to overcome underdevelopment.

The current stage of capitalism is marked by fierce disputes for the control and appropriation of water reserves, basic raw materials, rare earth minerals, energy sources, and biodiversity. Latin America is a privileged region for the offensives carried out by both imperialist economies and new economies with hegemonic aspirations with a view to obtaining such resources. Local capital, following a historical pattern, is willing to enter into agreements to dispose of these assets.

But imperialist capital's voracity is not limited to this kind of appropriation in dependent economies, to which we must add unequal exchange, the transfer of profits on investments, and interest payments on foreign debt. The plunder also extends to the operation of finance capital, which drains value (for example, by operating large pension funds); it involves pharmaceutical monopolies appropriating and patenting the knowledge of ancestral cultures; and it includes advanced laboratories and industries recruiting young researchers and scientists through scholarships and jobs.

The exploitation of millions of immigrants—many of them forced to remain undocumented or on temporary permits to reduce their wages and benefits—is not something alien to these processes. These people work in the fields during harvest, in construction, or in cleaning and other services, while their living labor is appropriated to enrich social reproduction in the imperialist economies.

At the beginning of research into dependency, the main concern was to identify processes that could account for the subordination of some economies to others that were characterized by their relatively stronger economic and political position in the international economy. From this perspective, special attention was given to foreign capital investments in the region; the extraction of profits; the absence or weakness of industrial branches and overall industrialization; and the lack of new technologies and technical knowledge, among other issues. These studies were what was first identified with dependency theory. Marxist theory and formation were not needed for its formulation and development; instead, the classical theories of international trade formed the basic point of departure.

However, a small group of researchers, starting from the assumption that Latin American economies and capital are subordinated to imperialist capital, would give a new "turn of the screw" by asking how dependent capital is reproduced in these conditions. They argued that its reproduction must be different from that taking place in the developed, imperialist world. To answer these questions, Marxist political economy and Marxism in general were key. Yet it was understood as a living theory capable of explaining new processes, which could not be limited to the simple repetition of formulas from the classic texts.

In our region, the Cuban Revolution has demonstrated the urgent need for a Marxism that is rigorous but reinvented to account for unprecedented phenomena. These, then, are some of the themes, problems, and approaches that gave rise to the Marxist theory of dependency.

Ruy Mauro Marini's great contributions, crystallized in the brief essay "The Dialectics of Dependency," consist in explaining how Latin America is inserted into the capitalist world system and how this leads to a particular form of capital reproduction. It is a form of reproduction sustained by super-exploitation, while accumulation is limited by unequal exchange and other transfers of value, and the productive apparatus remains far removed from the needs of the majority of the working population.

The processes and concepts formulated therein include elements that reach beyond the Latin American context. They also offer perspectives useful for studying the vast range of semicolonial and dependent economies in Africa and Asia.

For that reason, Marini's work has an internationalist dimension and represents a powerful contribution from Latin American Marxism to the struggles of the dispossessed and oppressed in other parts of the world. But it is also relevant to those who struggle inside present-day imperialism, which is strengthened by the intensified exploitation of the workers of dependent and semicolonial economies. Capitalism has ended up uniting the histories of the world's peoples, and with it, their struggles for emancipation.

—MEXICO CITY,
JULY 30, 2021

# Situating Ruy Mauro Marini (1932–1997): Movements, Struggles, and Intellectual Communities

## AMANDA LATIMER

*In theory, we assume that the laws of the capitalist mode of production develop in their pure form. In reality, this is only an approximation; but the approximation is all the more exact, the more the capitalist mode of production is developed and the less it is adulterated by survivals of earlier economic conditions with which it is amalgamated.*

—KARL MARX[1]

*The positive relationship between the increase in the productive capacity of labor and the greater exploitation of the worker, which becomes severe in the dependent economy, is not exclusive to the latter, but rather is generated by the capitalist mode of production itself.*

—RUY MAURO MARINI[2]

---

1. Karl Marx in Ruy Mauro Marini, "En torno a *Dialéctica de la dependencia*," in *Dialéctica de la dependencia* (Mexico, DF: Ediciones Era, 1973), 82.
2. Marini, "En torno a *Dialéctica*," 95.

## INTRODUCTION

In 2021, mass social struggles in Latin America offered hope to people fighting for a humane, dignified, and secure existence everywhere. At the time of writing, Colombia is in its fifth month of struggle against state-enforced impoverishment and state violence, directed particularly at its youth, while the Haitian working people have likewise been mobilized over the past two years, insisting that their country is more than a massive sweatshop for U.S. companies. Recently, Chilean citizens delivered a surprise victory for left and independent candidates (including seventeen Indigenous nominees) to a constituent assembly that will rewrite the 1980 constitution—a document that institutionalized the country's neoliberal model—potentially shattering the right-wing political establishment's hold over the country's bourgeois institutions for the first time in history. Finally, in Brazil, Ruy Mauro Marini's country of birth, outrage is growing against a far-right president and the sectors he represents, following the crass, destructive undervaluing of life that characterized the federal government's response to the Covid-19 crisis, which to date has left over 610,000 people dead.

The conditions in which Marxist dependency theory arose in the mid-1960s parallel those driving these contemporary revolts. Unsurprisingly, these conditions have contributed to a revival of interest in the dependency framework and its classic texts. In his preface to the first Brazilian edition of Ruy Mauro Marini's *Subdesarrollo y Revolución*, Nildo Ouriques argues that a new generation of scholars and movement intellectuals is returning to Marxist dependency theory because of the suffering of everyday people under a model of development that is not delivering for the majority. Ouriques also points to the degree to which the limits of neo-developmentalism and neo-structuralism are now clearly visible, echoing the crises of their earlier iterations in the mid-1960s. This has led to questions of what kind of development is possible in Brazil and Latin America more broadly, so long as the region is submitted to, not just neoliberalism, but capitalism and imperialism.

Ruy Mauro Marini was an intellectual giant of twentieth-century Marxism, having produced one of the most theoretically rich and rigorous accounts of capitalist development and underdevelopment in Latin America, at the heart of which he convincingly located labor super-exploitation. Despite his importance, Marini's work would remain unread and unavailable for much of the latter part of his life.[3] In Brazil, both Marini's writing and the Marxist approach to dependency theory more generally would be written out of the country's intellectual life. This situation persisted even following Marini's return to Brazil in 1984 after twenty years of exile, as a consequence of persistent authoritarianism and a rising neoliberal hegemony in the public sphere.

> Known in Europe, in the United States, and having immense prestige in the Spanish-speaking countries of Latin America for two decades, Ruy Mauro remained an author unknown to the new generations who attended university during the dictatorship (1964–1985). With the beginning of the democratic regime, many hoped that the country could begin not only a time of full freedom, which was shown to be necessary, but above all an intellectual renewal that, in the end, never occurred.[4]

The key issue, for Ouriques, is the degree to which the debate and analysis of class struggle would be weakened in Brazil due to the "systematic boycott" of Marini and of the Marxist dependency approach more generally during the neoliberal era.[5]

---

3. Cristóbal Kay writes: "Although Marini is, in my view, the most outstanding Marxist *dependentista* he is almost completely unknown in the English-speaking world." Cristóbal Kay, *Latin American Theories of Development and Underdevelopment* (London: Routledge, 1989), 144.
4. Nildo Ouriques, "Apresentação," in R. M. Marini, *Subdesenvolvimento e revolução*, trans. F. C. Prado & M. M. Gouvêa (Florianópolis, Brazil: Insular, 2012), 13.
5. As I began writing this essay, there were new episodes of censorship in Brazilian universities in the lead-up to the second round of the 2018 elections. Fernando Correa Prado, "Por qué hubo que desconocer a la teoría marxista de la dependencia en Brasil," in P. Olave, ed., *A 40 años de Dialéctica*

In academic settings of the Global North, it is true that dependency theory "reformed the academic and research curricula in many countries and began to shift the North-centric biases of the social sciences . . . helping to decolonize our minds."[6] However, it is also true that Northern debates on dependency, with no sense of irony, declared its "death" sometime during the launch of the latest round of globalization in the 1980s. Moreover, it was largely the reformist versions of dependency theory—popularized in English translations of the works of Fernando Henrique Cardoso with weaker grounding (if any) in Marxist theory—that were taken to represent the dependency thesis as a whole in the English-language debate.[7] Theotônio dos Santos aptly sums up the consequences of this oversight:

> Unfortunately . . . criticisms [of dependency theory] have not contributed much to the study of the problem as they reveal not only a great ignorance of the recent literature but also of the classic works on the situation of dependent countries. The resulting distortion has provoked a great deal of confusion over the concept of dependence, the relationship between dependency and imperialism, the existence of the dependency situation, the theoretical status of the concept, etcetera.[8]

Moreover, for English-speaking readers, lack of access to Ruy Mauro Marini's classic works and those of his contemporaries also impoverished the debate about class struggle and the world system in the Global North, I would argue, in the moment when we most needed

---

*de la dependencia* (Mexico, D.F.: Universidad Nacional Autónoma de México, Instituto de Investigaciones Económicas, 2015), 127–28; Cristóbal Kay, "Theotonio Dos Santos (1936–2018): the revolutionary intellectual who pioneered dependency theory," *Development and Change* 51, no. 2 (2020): 619.
6. Kay, "Theotonio dos Santos," 619.
7. For example, see Fernando Henrique Cardoso and Enzo Faletto, *Dependency and Development in Latin America*, trans. Marjory Mattingly Urquidi (Berkeley: University of California Press, 1979).
8. Kay, *Latin American Theories,* 163.

it: during the neoliberal phase of imperialism. Far from interpreting the realities of class struggle in Latin America alone, Marini's analytical framework brings into view the unity of the global working class. Many of his core works shed light on the ordering of workers at successive moments in the international division of labor, and their organization around different organic compositions of capital, and so, different forms and rates of exploitation.[9] They also shed light on the operation of the laws of capitalist accumulation (expressed theoretically in Marx's labor theory of value) across national boundaries.[10] The implications of these elements must be denaturalized and problematized before we are capable of fighting capitalism as a world system and the race to the bottom it requires. The super-exploitation that Marini identified as the foundation of dependent social formations is now clearly present in the precarious lives of workers in the Global North. As part of a global working class, it stands to reason that we should all be part of the same conversation.

It was once true that Marini, dos Santos, and Vânia Bambirra (and, to a lesser degree, Andre Gunder Frank) constituted a kind of "Marxism in exile" that was difficult to access for Latin Americans.[11] However, due to the dedication of a generation of their students, comrades, and colleagues, this state of affairs is now changing.[12] The majority of Marini's written work has been digitized and made available (where possible, in

9. Ruy Mauro Marini, *Dialéctica de la dependencia* (Mexico, D.F.: Ediciones Era, 1973); Ruy Mauro Marini, "Proceso y tendencias de la globalización capitalista," in Ruy Mauro Marini, *América Latina, dependencia y globalización: Fundamentos conceptuales Ruy Mauro Marini,* 2nd ed., coord. E. Sadir and T. dos Santos, ed. C. E. Martins and A. V. Sotelo (Bogotá, Colombia: CLACSO y Siglo del Hombre Editores, 1997), https://marini-escritos.unam.mx/?p=1531.

10. See Marini's own course material on Marx's *Capital.* Ruy Mauro Marini Escritos, "Cursos," https://marini-escritos.unam.mx/?cat=54.

11. Kay, *Latin American Theories,* 241n1.

12. Mathias Seibel Luce, *Teoria Marxista da Dependência: problemas e categorias—uma visão histórica* (São Paulo: Expressão Popular, 2018), 12.

multiple languages) at the online archive *Ruy Mauro Marini Escritos*, maintained by a team working under Jaime Osorio and hosted by the National Autonomous University of Mexico (UNAM).[13] Since 2000, many of Marini's key writings have been republished, including several in Portuguese for the first time. This includes the volume that sparked this project, *Ruy Mauro Marini—Vida e Obra*, edited by Roberta Traspadini and João Paulo Stedile, intellectuals associated with the Movimento dos Trabalhadores Sem Terra, and issued in 2005 by a publisher linked to Brazil's mass movements, Editora Expressão Popular in São Paulo.[14] Finally, as part of the bibliography for this recovery project, there are also publications shedding light on the systematic boycott of Marxist dependency theory in Brazil.[15]

Thankfully, with Marini's texts and ideas gaining greater attention in English as well, readers in the Global North now also have more access to his writings. There are a variety of contemporary works that adapt Marini's theoretical framework to the new conjuncture, and with the translations of his students' works, English-speaking readers can today join a vibrant and vital discussion with roots in Latin American social thought. The present translation of Marini's major work, *Dialéctica de la dependencia* (1973), is intended to be a key step in this direction, and I expect that it will not be the last.

The introduction that follows aims to put Ruy Mauro Marini's life and work in its social context. The span of his life covers some of the most intense periods of class struggle in Latin America's twentieth century. His life trajectory intersected with such important events as the crisis of dependent accumulation that culminated in the 1964 military coup in Brazil (which would drive Marini into exile for the first time); the democratic struggles waged by Mexican youth and workers in the

---

13. *Ruy Mauro Marini Escritos*, http://marini-escritos.unam.mx/.
14. Together with Escola Nacional Florestan Fernandes, Expressão Popular also produced a lively documentary about the author, *Ruy Mauro Marini e a Dialéctica da Dependência*, 2014, by Cecília Luedemann and Miguel Yoshida. The film features testimonies from many of the friends and comrades mentioned in this text, https://youtu.be/ww4_HoY-UYA.
15. Prado, "Por qué hubo que desconocer."

late 1960s that were brutally put down in the 1968 Tlatelolco Massacre; the intense class struggle that overtook Chile in the late 1960s, culminating in the rise of Salvador Allende and the Unidad Popular coalition (crushed in the September 11 coup d'état); the continent-wide rise of a new counterrevolutionary state and the maturing of the revolutionary left that opposed it, bolstered by the Cuban Revolution; and, finally, the struggles over the terms of redemocratization in Brazil in the shadow of the Washington Consensus, after twenty years of dictatorship. During all of this turmoil, Marini took part in revolutionary organizations throughout the continent. He transplanted his political focus following every new violent push into exile, but moved consistently in the direction common to the generation of 1968 in the Third World. That generation consistently positioned its pursuit of socialism in the particular histories and social composition of their respective social formations and, by necessary extension, in the worldwide struggle against imperialism.

> It was these tasks that drove him in the search for theoretical answers that could explain the current nature of the socialist revolution in Latin America, its perspectives, and the tasks that would make it possible. This forced him to move, like the great creators of Marxism, from complex theoretical reflection to revolutionary journalism and the formulating of slogans that sought to synthesize the tasks and demands needed to accumulate forces in a given period, along with relentless debate and critique of reformism, reaction, and counterrevolution.[16]

These experiences also gave rise to the questions that inspired Marxist dependency theory (MDT) in the work of Marini, dos Santos, Bambirra, Frank, and many others. This generation, despite finding itself steeped in developmentalist thought from the United States and Western Europe (mainly modernization theory and Keynesianism),

---

16. "Presentación," *Ruy Mauro Marini Escritos*, https://marini-escritos.unam.mx/.

would have to reckon with the question of why capitalist modernity, particularly as reflected in the developmental benchmarks of the United States and Britain, had failed to materialize at the periphery of the world system during the supposedly golden age of capitalism. This contradiction led to a crisis in the hegemony of imperialist thought that was only heightened by the triumph of the Cuban Revolution.[17]

Over the course of the late 1960s and '70s, Marini's generation would produce a new reading of Marx's historical materialism, the labor theory of value, and classical Marxist theories of imperialism— doing so from the perspective of dependent social formations, while attempting to make sense of their own realities.[18] They would examine the ways in which the Latin American economy had taken shape in accordance with world markets of the early modern era. This insertion in the world market gave rise to a particular, dependent form of capitalism, which saw the laws of accumulation modified in particular ways. Rather than being a deviation from a pure form of capitalist development, however, Marxist dependency theorists argued that "Latin American dependent capitalism is a mature capitalism that its originality is not due to the absence or lack of capitalism, but rather to the contrary."[19]

In what follows, I revisit Marini's seminal contributions to a series of debates that dominated Latin American social thought in the mid-twentieth century, including those with the region's traditional communist parties, the structuralist position of the UN's Economic Commission on Latin America (CEPAL, in its Spanish-language acronym), and the more reformist and Weberian strands of dependency theory developed by Fernando Henrique Cardoso. Over the course

---

17. Jaime Osorio, "El marxismo latinoamericano y la teoría de la dependencia," in *Teória marxista de la dependencia: Historia, fundamentos, debates y contribuciones* (Mexico City, D.F.: Universidad Autónoma Metropolitana (UAM)-Xochimilco, 2016), 54; Kay, *Latin American Theories*, 1–24.

18. Theotonio dos Santos in Kay, *Latin American Theories*, 143.

19. Jaime Osorio, *Teória marxista de la dependencia: Historia, fundamentos, debates y contribuciones* (Mexico City: Universidad Autónoma Metropolitana (UAM)-Xochimilco, 2016), 9.

of his sixty-five years, Marini would produce a vast range of written material including: five books (published in at least seven languages, in various editions around the world); over 80 academic articles, investigative reports, and conference papers; at least 200 newspaper articles, while working as a journalist in Brazil, Chile, Mexico, and as a correspondent for Cuba; and a variety of editorials and reports of the diverse revolutionary groups in which he took part.[20] The incredibly rich theoretical and methodological framework that Marini developed grew out of a rich social context involving the practical deliberations and programmatic articulations of revolutionary tendencies, contact with a variety of living anticolonial movements for self-determination, fertile discussions with students and colleagues in a variety of academic settings, and long-curated friendships, stretching over decades, that were embedded in transformational politics.

To situate Marini in the varied social contexts that shaped him and his work, I have leaned heavily on his own memoir: an extensive autobiographical statement written in August 1990 in the effort to be readmitted to the University of Brasília's faculty after a twenty-six-year enforced absence.[21] Not only was this text indispensable to understanding the author's intellectual, political, and (to a certain extent) personal trajectory, but this essay also takes its direction from one of the author's early comments therein: "I am very much the product of deep tendencies that have determined the rise of modern Brazil."[22] The essay uses tributes and testimonials written by former students, friends, and comrades following Marini's death in 1997. This includes Vânia Bambirra and, indirectly, Theotonio dos Santos, major forces behind the development of Marxist dependency theory in their own right, both of whom were lost in recent years, in 2015 and 2018 respectively. Finally,

---

20. Translations of material from these texts in what follows (and errors therein) are my own. Please see the Translator's Note in this volume.

21. Ruy Mauro Marini, "Memória: por Ruy Mauro Marini," in *Ruy Mauro Marini—vida e obra,* ed. R. Traspadini and J. P. Stedile (São Paulo: Expressão Popular, 2005), 57–134. The memoir is also available in Spanish at Ruy Mauro Marini Escritos, "Memoria," https://marini-escritos.unam.mx/?page_id=348.

22. Ibid., 57.

the essay will touch on key turning points in the author's thought that mirrored the variety of roles he played in life, each enriching the next.[23]

## BEGINNINGS: 1932-1960

Ruy Mauro de Araújo Marini was born on May 2, 1932, in Barbacena, a small city in the southeastern state of Minas Gerais, to parents who were only one generation away from the land on either side, albeit from different ends of the social spectrum. His father's parents had emigrated to Brazil from Italy in the eventful year of 1888, when Brazil became the last country in the Western Hemisphere to abolish slavery. By contrast, his mother's family were large landowners in Minas Gerais whose fortunes had declined following that same milestone in Brazilian history, the abolition of slavery.

At age eighteen, Marini relocated to nearby Rio de Janeiro, intending to study medicine. Three years later, however, he entered the law faculty at the University of Brazil (today, the Federal University of Rio de Janeiro). In this setting, he soon became swept up in the intense debates over nationalism and development that dominated public discourse throughout the 1950s, finding himself drawn to the communist position.[24] During his time in Rio, Marini expanded his command of languages. Having already had basic instruction in Latin, Portuguese, and Brazilian literature in Barbacena, he now turned to studying English, French, and Spanish. In 1955, he entered the newly formed Escola Brasileira da Administração Pública (Brazilian School of Public Administration) to study social sciences for the first time. There he encountered a generally young cohort of instructors who stood out

---

23. Nelson Gutiérrez summed up this dialectic between thought and revolutionary activity in Marini's life with these words: "Ruy lived as a prisoner of the dilemma between his natural inclinations as a builder of knowledge, thinker, and theoretician, and his responsibility as a man of action, a political subject, geared to the task of changing existing social relations." Nelson Gutiérrez Y., "Ruy Mauro Marini: perfil de um intelectual revolucionário," in Traspadini and Stedile, *Ruy Mauro Marini—vida e obra*, 263–81.

24. Marini, "Memória," 60.

against the "traditionalist and rarefied intellectual climate" that dominated the universities of the day.[25]

Among those who left a mark on Marini was the sociologist Alberto Guerreiro Ramos. Ramos's thinking, particularly regarding the role of intellectuals and technical management and planning in industrial development, was being transformed at that time by the developmentalist discourse of CEPAL and the 1955 Conference at Bandung.[26] In the same year, Ramos became a founding faculty member at the Instituto Superior de Estudos Brasileiros (Higher Institute of Brazilian Studies, ISEB), a center that would later become famous for its focus on nationalism and development.[27] In his work, Ramos referred to the concept of dependency, albeit from the perspective of a national bourgeoisie that was dependent on the development paradigm coming out of the United States. In a 1956 text, the author "argued for the liberation of the bourgeoisie from its semicolonial and underdeveloped mentality to one that was oriented to the country's development."[28] Hence, the concept of dependency may not have had the theoretical elaboration it would receive at the hand of Marini's generation, but it was certainly part of the period's intellectual climate.

As it turned out, Marini would leave Brazil just as the structuralist approach to development, set in motion by CEPAL, was reaching its peak.[29] With encouragement from Ramos, Marini entered Sciences Po,

---

25. Ibid.

26. Ronald Chilcote, *Intellectuals and the Search for National Identity in Twentieth-Century Brazil* (Cambridge: Cambridge University Press, 2018), 10, 28.

27. Chilcote, *Intellectuals*, 57–125.

28. Ibid., 60.

29. According to Kay, structuralism came about as a response to neoclassical economics and monetarism which, along with Keynesianism, dominated development theory in the postwar era. In an effort to understand endemic underdevelopment, Latin American development specialists began questioning the usefulness of such frameworks and stressing "the specificity of the peripheral countries" in the world system as they searched for a new paradigm that could explain their "structures, dynamics, and realities." Structuralists, whose thought was inspired by CEPAL, were so named due to their focus on historical and structural analysis.

the Paris Institute of Political Studies, to study sociology on a grant from the French government in September 1958. Over the next year and a half, Marini would complete his political formation—as much through travels in Europe and encounters with people from around the world, as through systematic study of Marx, Hegel, and particularly Lenin.[30] Crucially, Marini immersed himself in the fervent political debates taking place around him in Europe. At the same time, he paid careful attention to the challenges to the very terms of those debates posed by young exiles from the anticolonial struggles in Vietnam, Cambodia, Algeria, and parts of sub-Saharan Africa. Exposure to these debates would make him more critical of the dominant development paradigms of the day. Reflecting on the impact of his time in France, Marini would later write:

> The theories of development so in vogue in the United States and in European centers were revealed to me as what they really were: an instrument of mystification and domestication of the oppressed peoples of the Third World and a weapon with which imperialism sought to confront the problems created in the postwar period by decolonization.[31]

However, it was the short period to come, at home, that would see this

---

They rejected the methodological individualism of orthodox economics along with, notably, neoclassical trade theory and Ricardo's theory of comparative advantage. Kay, *Latin American Theories,* 2–5, 47, 228–29; see also Ana Garcia and Miguel Borba de Sá, "Brazil: From the margins to the centre?" in *The Essential Guide to Critical Development Studies*, ed. H. Veltmeyer and P. Bowles (London: Routledge, 2018), 386. Rather than seeking to overcome dependency as such, the structuralist solution was "to know under what conditions more dividends could be gained from participating" in the international system. Garcia and Sá, "Brazil," 386; see also Kay, *Latin American Theories,* 127. In what follows, I will look at how Marxist dependency theory responded to features of structuralist thought, including structural dualism and the effects of deteriorating terms of trade between the core and periphery. See Kay, *Latin American Theories,* 25–57.
30. Marini, "Memória," 62.
31. Ibid., 62–63.

sharpened critique of mainstream development thinking culminate in political praxis; a period that would end abruptly with Marini's first expulsion into exile.

## BRAZIL: 1960-1964

In mid-1960, Marini returned to Rio de Janeiro to take a position at the Institute for Retirement and Pensions of Industrial Workers, IAPI. At the same time, as a journalist, he began to enter the major debates taking place in the revolutionary left, producing articles for revolutionary Cuba's newly formed press agency, *Prensa Latina*, and for *O Metropolitano*, the outlet of the National Union of Students.[32] In this role, one that he would return to throughout his life, Marini covered major historical events of the day, including the anticolonial struggles taking place worldwide and the key episodes in Brazilian class struggle. Among the latter were the 1961 National Congress of Peasants in Belo Horizonte, and the mass struggle waged by the Peasant Leagues under the leadership of Francisco Julião (the antecedent of the landless workers movements that would erupt a decade later). Marini considered the Peasant Leagues struggle to be one of the highlights of revolutionary activity in this period, all the more so due to the ideological battle it provoked with the Brazilian Communist Party (Partido Comunista Brasileiro, or PCB). In the pages of *O Metropolitano*, Marini worked to make what he called this "silent struggle"—far from the eye of the bourgeois press—explicit, in original stories that illustrated "the development of the ideological and political struggle then underway."[33]

In September 1962, Marini joined the University of Brasília, working initially as a teaching assistant and, a year later, as an associate professor. He later wrote that this was one of the most intellectually fulfilling periods of his academic life.[34] The university had been founded only two years earlier, in the same year that Brasília became the new

---

32. Marini's journalistic writings are available at *Ruy Mauro Marini Escritos*, https://marini-escritos.unam.mx/?page_id=3692.
33. Marini, "Memória," 64.
34. Ibid., 65.

capital of the republic. Under the direction of anthropologist Darcy Ribeiro, the University of Brasília sought to break from the traditional university mold with "progressive curricula, research and teaching methods."[35] More important, however, was the vibrant and talented cohort of intellectuals Marini would meet there, several of whom became lifelong friends, interlocutors, and comrades. They included German-American sociologist Andre Gunder Frank—whose ideas on development and underdevelopment would be deeply influenced by his time in Brazil—and, even more critically, Theotonio dos Santos and Vânia Bambirra. It was inside this "polemical trio" that the germs of Marxist dependency theory started to take shape, first in the context of a reading group on Marx's *Capital* and exchanges in Brasília, and later in exile in Chile and Mexico.[36]

These debates extended beyond the university campus. Even prior to his return, Marini entered into contact with militants of Socialist Youth (Juventude Socialista), the youth wing of the Brazilian Socialist Party (Partido Socialista Brasileiro, PSB). This group had entered into the debate surrounding the crisis of the late 1950s with a strong critique of the Kubitschek government.[37] Moreover, within months of his return from France, Marini joined the Guanabara (Rio de Janeiro) section of Juventude Socialista and participated in the formation of a new group, the Revolutionary Marxist Organization-Workers Politics (ORM-PO, Organização Revolucionária Marxista-Política Operária, better known as POLOP, after its main publication). Also participating in this new formation were dos Santos, Bambirra, and Juarez Guimarães de Brito, all of Labor Youth (Mocidade Trabalhista, a current of the Partido Trabalhista Brasileiro, or Brazilian Labor Party) from Minas Gerais; Eder and Emir Sader, Michael Löwy, and others from the Independent Socialist League (Liga Socialista Independente) in São Paulo; Aluízio

35. Kay, "Theotonio Dos Santos," 602.
36. Sadi Dal Rosso and Raphael Lana Seabra, "A teoria marxista da dependência: papel e lugar das ciências sociais da Universidade de Brasília," *Revista Sociedade e Estado* 31 (2017): 1029–50.
37. Passa Palavra, "Extrema-esquerda e desenvolvimento" (series), parts 8 and 9, June 2011, https://passapalavra.info/2011/06/95903/.

Leite Filho, Simon Schwartzman, and others from the student movement at the Brazilian School of Public Administration (EBAP) in Rio;
and two groups from the northeastern state of Bahía.[38]

POLOP was the first expression of the revolutionary left to emerge in
Brazil.[39] It also provided a collective space of theorization, as reflected
in Marini's earliest theoretical output.[40] The tendency came together
around a reading of Brazilian society that cut against the grain of
dominant left frameworks—a reading born of disillusionment with the
populist slogans of national unity and developmentalism. This critique
emerged following the breakup of the class alliance that had sustained
the bourgeois system of domination since the Vargas era of the 1930s.
In the words of Erich Sachs, one of the current's intellectuals with
whom Marini would develop a deep friendship, a new framework was
needed to expose "the penetration of developmentalist ideas in the
working class, facilitated by a skillful exploitation of the reigning anti-
imperialist feelings among the masses."[41] In an effort to neutralize any
organized opposition to its class interests, the dominant bloc had ral-
lied the working class behind the ideology of developmentalism:

> [The dominant bloc] knew how to take advantage of this movement,
> when it found it useful, in order to improve its position in the alliance
> that it had maintained with imperialism—where it is relegated to the

38. Daniel Aarão Reis F. and Jair Ferreira de Sá, eds., "Organização Revolucionária
Marxista-Política Operária—ORM-POLOP," in *Imagens da Revolução: documentos políticos das organizações clandestinas de esquerda dos anos 1961 a 1971* (Rio
de Janeiro: Editora Marco Zero, 1985); Theotonio dos Santos, quoted in Passa
Palavra, "Extrema-esquerda."

39. Marini, "Memória," 62.

40. See for example Ruy Mauro Marini, "La dialéctica del desarrollo capitalista en
Brasil," *Cuadernos Americanos* 146, no. 3 (1966), https://marini-escritos.unam.
mx/?p=1126; Orlando Miranda and Pery Falcón, eds., *POLOP: uma trajetória
de luta pela organização independente da classe operária no Brasil—2ª edição*
(Salvador, Brazil: Centro de Estudos Victor Meyer, 2010).

41. Erich Sachs, in Raphael Lana Seabra, "A vocação política da teoria marxista
da dependência: uma análise da Política Operária," *Latin American Research
Review* 55, no. 4 (2020): 665.

role of "poor cousin." . . . The problem of the anti-imperialist struggle as posed by the so-called left, reinforces the apparent community of interests [between the working class and national bourgeoisie], and once again justifies the sacrifices [demanded of] the proletariat.[42]

POLOP's framework took direct aim at the strategy of class conciliation championed by the Brazilian Communist Party, which sought an alliance between the native bourgeoisie and the working classes in order to stabilize Brazil's industrial development. For example, the following observation appears in the document "Perspectives on the class struggle in Brazil," approved at the second congress of POLOP in 1963, which Raphael Seabra suggests roughly foreshadows Marini's conceptualization of super-exploitation:[43]

The rejection of all bourgeois and reformist attempts to structure "alliances" between the proletariat, the national bourgeoisie, and certain sectors of allegedly anti-imperialist landowners. Such attempts do nothing but . . . hide the fact that the Brazilian worker is victim of a double exploitation, that of the national capitalist and that of the foreign one which, in disputing their shares of surplus value, deprive the anti-imperialist struggle of its class character.[44]

POLOP also called for a grounded Marxist analysis of the core social relations in Brazil that would clarify the character of the revolution needed in the country. The tendency criticized the communist parties' efforts to import revolutionary models wholesale, which implied that all countries were on the same universal path toward capitalist modernity, with some deviations from this path understood as "shortcomings and others as deformations."[45] In this regard, POLOP recognized that Brazil was already a "mature capitalist country and not a semicolonial

---

42. Ibid.
43. Ibid., 662n1.
44. POLOP in Seabra, "A vocação política," 668.
45. Ibid., 665.

one as per the PCB [Communist Party] thesis."[46] Brazil needed a socialist revolution, meaning that it would have to be simultaneously anti-imperialist and anticapitalist, led by an independent party of the working class—a role that existing parties had so far failed to play.[47]

It is important to stress that POLOP's politics cannot be reduced to an early expression of Marxist dependency theory, nor was the latter ever formally adopted by the tendency, possibly due to its originating members' diverse political backgrounds.[48] Nevertheless, Seabra manages to identify fundamental ideas and categories that appear in POLOP's resolutions, directives, and eventual political program, forged in the "heat of political battle in Brazil between 1959 and 1967," which would later be elaborated upon in the initial works of Marini, dos Santos, and Bambirra during their exile.[49] For example, the group appealed to the concept of "antagonistic cooperation" that later became important in Marini's conceptualization of subimperialism (to be discussed below).

Years later, Marini would situate the roots of Marxist dependency theory in debates within the "new left" in Brazil. He strongly rejected the conflation of this new vision with the PCB's recycling of CEPAL's developmentalist positions, which foregrounded a nationalist bourgeoisie as the subject of transformation.[50] Marini writes that the PCB

leaned toward the Cepaline thesis of the deterioration of the terms of trade, structural dualism and the *viability of autonomous capitalist development*, to support the principle of democratic-bourgeois, anti-imperialist and anti-feudal revolution that they had inherited from the Third International. Positioning itself against this, the "new left" characterized the revolution as simultaneously anti-imperialist and

46. Luiz Alberto Moniz Bandeira, quoted in Passa Palavra, "Extrema-esquerda."
47. Seabra, "A vocação política," 663.
48. Seabra observes that there is only one mention of "dependency" in early texts of the current, appearing in relation to the "limits of productivity [under] imperialism due to the 'low levels of consumption in dependent areas.'" Ibid., 666.
49. Ibid., 662.
50. Marini, "Memória"; see also Gutiérrez, "Ruy Mauro Marini," 264.

socialist, rejecting the idea of the dominance of feudal relations in the countryside and denying that the Latin American bourgeoisie had the capacity to direct the anti-imperialist struggle.[51]

The economic and political crisis facing the country came to a head in the early 1960s. It involved, on the one hand, the radicalization of urban and rural workers, whom the left struggled to keep pace with. On the other, there was big capital's reactionary backlash against the modest "basic reforms" that left-populist president João Goulart had proposed in an attempt to stabilize the country (*reformas de base*, including banking, tax, urban, electoral, university, and crucially, agrarian reforms, as well as changes in the status of foreign capital).[52] Anticipating the coming coup, POLOP observed that "the contradictions that were deepening and accelerating in Brazil were results of capitalist development itself."[53] The tendency claimed that these contradictions could only be met through a revolutionary alliance between subaltern classes in the countryside and cities.[54] While recognizing that "the history of Latin America . . . is divided into two phases: before and after the Cuban revolution," Marini explains in his 1990 memoir that

the development of the Brazilian and Latin American revolutionary left (particularly in Argentina, in Peru, in Venezuela and in Nicaragua) was not, as is often purported, an effect of the Cuban Revolution, but part of the same process that gave rise to it—no matter how strongly its influence was felt in the 1960s.[55]

POLOP eventually developed an internal rift—over the question of

---

51. Marini, "Memória," 66.
52. Seabra, "A vocação política," 668n9; Luiz Alberto Moniz Bandeira, *O governo João Goulart: as lutas sociais no Brasil—1961-1964*, 7th ed. (Rio de Janeiro: Editora Revan, Editora UnB, 2001).
53. Seabra, "A vocação política," 670; see also Bandeira, *O governo*, 81–86.
54. Miranda and Falcón, *POLOP*, 33.
55. Marini, "Memória," 63.

whether to turn to armed struggle—which triggered the exit of dos Santos, who was then the movement's acting General Secretary.[56]

For his part, in addition to his teaching duties, Marini had begun work on a doctoral thesis exploring the legacy of bonapartist (or populist) authoritarianism under both the Quadros (in 1961) and Goulart governments.[57] On April 1, 1964, the first day of the coup, a military invasion of the University of Brasília resulted in the destruction of the material he had developed to date. Marini then fled to Rio, only to discover that he had been dismissed from the university by military decree, along with a dozen other academics.[58] Over the next three months, Marini would be arrested twice. First, the Naval Intelligence Center detained and tortured him. After he was released on a *habeas corpus* order by the nominally independent Federal Supreme Court, he was kidnapped once again by the Brazilian marines and held by the army.[59] Released in December 1964, Marini remained underground for three months until, with constant pressure on his family and attacks on his comrades, he was granted asylum in Mexico.[60]

---

56. Kay, "Theotonio dos Santos," 602.

57. Dal Rosso and Seabra, *"A teoria marxista da dependência,"* 1046.

58. From 2012 to 2015, the University of Brasília organized the Anísio Teixeira Commission on Truth and Memory to investigate the civil and human rights violations that took place at the university between 1964 and 1985. The commission was named after one of Marini's comrades, who, as rector, was removed from office and murdered by the regime in 1971. See Universidade de Brasília, "Comissão Anísio Teixeira de Memória e Verdade," http://www.comissaoverdade.unb.br.

59. Patricia Olave, "Ruy Mauro Marini: mínima cronología," in P. Olave, ed., *A 40 años de Dialéctica de la dependencia* (Mexico, D.F.: Universidad Nacional Autónoma de México, Instituto de Investigaciones Económicas, 2015), 12–13.

60. POLOP took part in an armed urban struggle, which failed, resulting in the persecution, death, and disappearance of several comrades, including Juarez Guimarães de Brito. Kay, "Theotonio dos Santos," 603. In 1971, Marini wrote an essay contextualizing and critiquing POLOP's armed struggle. He wrote the text for a two-volume series, edited by Vânia Bambirra, that critically evaluated regional movements inspired by the Guevarista *foco theory*. Ruy Mauro Marini, "La izquierda revolucionario brasileña y las nuevas condiciones de la lucha de clases," in *Diez Años de Insurreción en América Latina,* vol. 2, ed. V. Bambirra (Santiago, Chile: Editorial Prensa Latinoamericana S.A., 1971), 113–66. The chapter would

## FIRST EXILE: MEXICO, 1964–1969

| | |
|---|---|
| *La patria no es el amor* | The homeland is not love |
| *La patria no es el cuerpo* | The homeland is not the body |
| *La patria son los hijos* | The homeland is the children |
| *La patria eres tú* | The homeland is you |
| *La patria es el trabajo* | The homeland is work |
| *La mano que hace el pan* | The hand that makes bread |
| *El grito valeroso que rompe la* | The courageous cry that breaks |
|  *cadenas* |  chains |
| *La alma de los barrios,* | The souls of the barrios |
| *La joven compañera* | The young compañera |
| *La muerte tempranera del joven* | The premature death of a young |
|  *luchador,* |  fighter |
| *La madre que los espera llorando* | The mother who waits for him |
|  *con rencor.* |  weeping with bitterness. |
| | |
| *Amigo ven* | Come, friend |
| *Te voy a dar . . .* | And I will give you . . . |
| *Mi parecer, amiga.* | My opinion, friend. |

—From "Amigo Ven," by León Chávez Teixeiro, musician, filmmaker, and organizer in the Mexican workers movement who chronicled the mass upsurge of the 1960s

At age thirty-two, Marini arrived in Mexico and became part of a community of Brazilian academics and comrades, many of whom were also experiencing exile for the first time. He would later identify these four short years as the period in which he came into his own professionally.[61] During this time, Marini crafted a novel conceptual framework for understanding the nature and implications of the Brazilian coup. In texts that reflected his growing relationship with radical student

---

reappear in the fifth edition of *Subdesarrollo y Revolución* as "Lucha armada y lucha de clases." Ruy Mauro Marini, *Subdesarrollo y Revolución*, 5th ed. (Mexico, D.F.: Siglo XXII Editores, 1974), 141–90.

61. Marini, "Memória," 83.

movements in Brazil and Mexico, he also analyzed how the organized left and the student movement pushed back against the Brazilian dictatorship.

In his new home, Marini's name started to become recognized in local intellectual circles and institutions, and eventually, internationally. He joined the Center for International Studies at the Colégio de México, first as part of the editorial board of its flagship journal, *Foro Internacional,* and from 1966 onward, as head of the program in international relations. In mid-1966, Marini took a position at Conescal, the Regional Center of School Buildings for Latin America, a joint organ of UNESCO, the OAS, and the Mexican government. There, he broadened the scope of his studies of Latin America's social and economic realities, including research into its burgeoning student movements.[62]

Finally, in 1968, Marini joined the Center for Latin American Studies (Centro de Estudos Latino-Americanos, or CELA) at the Universidad Nacional Autónoma de México (UNAM). He would remain associated with CELA until the end of his life, with many of his former students eventually becoming associates, interlocutors, and co-investigators.[63] In 1969, Marini was forced into exile for a second time.

### On the Origins of the Brazilian Dictatorship

In 1965, with a report delivered to the POLOP Central Committee, Marini began work on a series of texts dealing with both the roots of the Brazilian coup and its startling aftermath.[64] What emerged following this event was a new "total economic-political scheme" that aimed to resolve the crisis of the late 1950s and early '60s through a state formation that "put a definitive stamp of approval on the fusion of military and big capital interests." This formation included a new political economy that Marini labeled *subimperialism.* He referred to it as "the form that dependent capitalism assumes upon reaching

---

62. Ibid., 77–78.
63. Ibid., 69–77; Ana Esther Ceceña, "Ruy Mauro Marini: um construtor de caminhos," in Traspadini and Stedile, *Ruy Mauro Marini—vida e obra*, 289–302.
64. Marini, "Memória," 70.

the stage of monopolies and finance capital."[65] Several of these essays would be gathered in Marini's first book, *Subdesarrollo y Revolución* (Underdevelopment and Revolution), and published in 1969 by the newly formed publishing house Siglo XXI.[66] Even so, his painstaking analysis of Brazilian capitalism's development and class struggle in the country continued to evolve in keeping with the regime itself.

Initially, Marini's objective was to counter the prevailing line that blamed the coup on U.S. imperialism alone: "a body foreign . . . to the internal logic of Brazilian life." This was a discourse that erased the interests, actions, and culpability of the Brazilian bourgeoisie.[67] In "La dialéctica del desarrollo capitalista en Brasil" (initially published in the Mexican journal *Cuadernos Americanos* in 1966, and later reissued in expanded form in *Subdesarrollo y Revolución*), Marini locates the events of 1964 in a new interpretation of Brazilian development during its modern era.[68] The dominant reading of this period, which opens with the 1937 populist dictatorship of Getúlio Vargas, usually attributes the roots of Brazilian underdevelopment to two elements: (1) a structurally dualist economy, split between modern industry and a still backward and semi-feudal agrarian system; and (2) a class structure dominated by the traditional oligarchy and U.S. imperialism that sidelined the incipient industrial bourgeoisie. A year into the military regime, proponents of this interpretation (largely the PCB and left nationalists) looked forward to the resumption of a bourgeois democratic revolution that echoed the rise of the national bourgeoisies in Europe's classical industrial revolutions. Their strategy involved a united front of the bourgeoisie and working classes.

For Marini, however, this approach ignored the actual role that large fractions of industrial and finance capital and sections of the

---

65. Ruy Mauro Marini, "Brazilian Subimperialism," *Monthly Review* 23, no. 2 (1972): 15.

66. Marini, *Subdesarrollo*.

67. Marini, "Memória," 69.

68. Marini, "La dialéctica del desarrollo"; Marini, "Memória," 72; see also Chilcote, *Intellectuals*, 173–203.

petit bourgeoisie played in the 1964 coup.[69] Essentially, it elided the
major developments of the modern era. During that period there was
no antagonistic divide between backward and modern sectors; in fact,
industrialization had occurred based on the complementary interests
of industrial capital and the traditional rural oligarchy. There was a
holding pattern of compromise between these two groups, however
fractious it could be at times. This compromise broke down in the
1950s, spurred by a fall in key agricultural exports and their prices
on international markets. Falling prices reduced the foreign exchange
available to purchase the capital goods needed for industry and led to
continuous bottlenecks in the sale of commodities (particularly durable goods that were produced by monopoly sectors) due to the limited
size of the domestic market.[70] In other words, it was essentially a crisis
of realization.[71]

   In the same decade, any opportunity for the bourgeoisie to act more
autonomously in pursuit of national development was undermined
by a shift in U.S. imperialism, as direct investment (or FDI) began to
penetrate key sectors of manufacturing.[72] Rather than alleviating the
social contradictions inherent to the system, the introduction of new
technology in the late 1950s sharpened the crisis faced by workers and
unleashed a new cycle of social polarization based on the general law of
accumulation.[73] In the wake of higher productivity, labor was increasingly displaced from industrial sectors dominated by big capital, which
resulted in widespread impoverishment. Meanwhile, in the rural sector,
increased mechanization and a fall in exports led to a similar wave of
displacement. With neither the countryside nor the urban centers able
to absorb the surplus labor, the crisis generated mass struggles on both
fronts. In the countryside, the Peasant Leagues demanded agrarian

69. Marini, "La dialéctica del desarrollo."

70. Ruy Mauro Marini, "Brazilian Interdependence and Imperialist Integration,"
*Monthly Review* 17, no. 7 (1965): 10–23, 26–29.

71. Marini, "Brazilian subimperialism," 15–16.

72. Marini, "La dialéctica del desarrollo."

73. See chapter 25 of Karl Marx, *Capital: A Critique of Political Economy*, vol. 1,
trans. Ben Fowkes (London: Penguin Books, 1990).

reform. In the cities, trade unions fought for wage increases to help workers cope with food shortages and inflation.

The industrial bourgeoisie attempted to manage these pressures under (and through) three different administrations. The last was the Goulart government (1961–64), which tried to revive a "bourgeois-worker united front, of Varguista inspiration, [but] this time backed by the communists."[74] Each attempt failed. Facing intensified class conflict and a falling rate of profit, the bourgeoisie finally opted for a military solution: the April 1964 coup.

### Subimperialism

In a 1965 article published in *Monthly Review*, Marini attempts to contextualize the coup by exploring its economic and class-related causes at a regional level, but also tries to make sense of the regime's economic and military ambitions in the region. These ambitions were somewhat autonomous but still took place under the aegis of U.S. imperialism.[75] Marini would call this strategy *subimperialism*, and, as mentioned earlier, he located its origins in key, interrelated developments in the postwar period that eventually contributed to "integration" with imperialism. First, inside the United States, there was a growth of monopolies and, along with it, the increase of capital surpluses that the domestic economy was unable to absorb. These, in turn, became outward-going direct investments. Second, inside Brazil, there were the dynamics of FDI and worker displacement (discussed above). Third, there was an increasing integration of military ideology, aid, training, and support taking place at a regional level. This integration exemplified what the Brazilian geopolitical ideologue General Golbery do Couto e Silva termed the "loyal bargain" (*barganha leal*), or the doctrine of continental integration, which proposed Brazil's acquiescence to U.S. national security policy.[76] Marini explained the bargain this way:

---

74. Marini, "La dialéctica del desarrollo."
75. Marini, "Brazilian interdependence"; Marini, "Memória," 72.
76. The U.S. national security doctrine of the time involved extending the national security apparatus and its domestic war against communist "subversion"

Brazil cannot escape North American influence . . . no alternative remains but to "consciously accept the mission of associating ourselves with the policy of the United States in the South Atlantic." The counterpart of this "conscious choice" would be the recognition by the United States that "the quasi-monopoly of rule in that area should be exercised by Brazil exclusively."[77]

In this context, in 1965, Brazilian troops took part in the U.S. intervention against the progressive nationalist government of Coronel Francisco Caamaño in the Dominican Republic.[78] However, Marini balks at the suggestion that the Brazilian coup had relegated Brazil to being a mere vassal of the United States. "What we have, in reality, is the evolution of the Brazilian bourgeoisie toward the conscious acceptance of its integration with North American imperialism, an evolution resulting from the very logic of the economic and political dynamics of Brazil."[79] In other words, far from being driven simply by geopolitical ideology and ambition, the roots of this strategy derive from the structural contradictions—the irrational or peculiar character—of Brazil's dependent capitalism, which sets it apart from classical industrial development. These contradictions made Brazil unable to control its technological progress or create the domestic markets it requires, leading to the pauperization of the majority of Brazilians, even to the point of stunting the country's further capitalist expansion.[80]

Building on the concept of "antagonistic cooperation," Marini argues that the bourgeoisie has opted for a strategy of subimperialism

---

to the rest of the Western Hemisphere. This was done partly through the Treaty of Rio de Janeiro (1947), which ratified "collaboration with the United States in a global anticommunist strategy, to the extent of justifying military intervention in any country threatened or conquered by 'communist penetration.'" Benjamin Keen and Keith Haynes, *A History of Latin America*, 8th ed. (London: Wadsworth CENGAGE, 2009), 309.

77. Marini, "Brazilian interdependence," 20.
78. Keen and Haynes, *A History*, 309.
79. Marini, "Brazilian interdependence," 21.
80. Marini, "La dialéctica del desarrollo."

in the region to compensate for the limits to capital accumulation imposed by both the pact with U.S. imperialism and the antiquated agrarian system.[81] Subimperialism works to compensate for these tendencies by opening regional markets for Brazilian industrial exports (including the products of a growing military-industrial complex) in a way that complements the expansion of U.S. multinationals rather than directly competing with them.[82]

However, rather than resolving the structural contradictions that produced Brazilian dependency, the policy merely reproduces them. The subimperialist pact also allows (mostly U.S.) monopoly capital to enter into and dominate key industrial sectors while helping to generate, partly through state terror and repression, extraordinary profits that are shared by the biggest fractions of the Brazilian and imperialist bourgeoisies. Thus, "foreign capital is provided with the internal conditions for expanding investment and profits in Brazil in return for access to advanced technology and the world market controlled by the monopolies of the developed countries."[83]

Nor does the subimperialist pact benefit the Brazilian working class. While the productive apparatus of certain industrial sectors undergoes a

---

81. Seabra examines the role of this concept in "A Socialist Programme for Brazil," a document issued by POLOP in September 1967. Seabra, "A vocação política." Coined by German Marxist August Thalheimer, the term "antagonistic cooperation" refers to a dynamic of the imperialist system formed during and after the two World Wars. A POLOP program describes it as follows: "a cooperation aimed at the conservation of the system and which has its basis in the very process of capital centralization, and which does not eliminate the antagonisms inherent in the imperialist world. Cooperation prevails and will prevail over antagonisms." POLOP, "Programa Socialista Para o Brasil (September 1967)," in Reis F. and Sá, "Organização," 91–92. In POLOP's view, antagonistic cooperation is what bound the national bourgeoisies of underdeveloped countries to those of imperialist countries. The aim was to "ensure the continuity of imperialist exploitation after the withdrawal of colonial armies." Ibid., 93; see also Seabra, "A vocação política," 668–69.

82. Garcia and Sá, "Brazil," 388.

83. Kay, *Latin American Theories*, 148.

rise in the organic composition of capital, it does so to perverse effect.[84] Throughout the years of the "Brazilian Miracle" (from 1968 onward, coinciding with an intensification of state terror), wage suppression and the absorption of small and medium firms contributed to income concentration and to the subsequent development of, firstly, a consumer market for high-end luxury products for the middle and upper classes, and, secondly, to the production of capital and durable consumer goods for the state itself (to upgrade military armaments and for use in infrastructure and megaprojects). Both developments were deliberately (and monstrously, in the author's own words) ill-fitted to the masses' consumer needs.[85] In this way, subimperialism—"imperialism without the generalized capitalist transformation of the economy"—and super-exploitation are understood by Marini to be deeply linked.[86]

With these arguments, Marini challenges a popular thesis about the unviability of development under the dictatorship. This was the so-called pastoralization thesis of economist Celso Furtado, one of the most prominent proponents of structuralism in Brazil.[87] Furtado suggested that the domination of foreign capital would lead to the stagnation of import-substituting industrialization, displacing national capital to the countryside, and thus forcing the country to return to its former role as an exporter of primarily agricultural goods. By contrast, Marini's position was that "the dictatorship corresponded to the domination of big national and foreign capital and propelled the economy to a higher stage of capitalist development," but that it did so by deepening the contradictions already present in the system.[88]

Marini concludes that his interpretation allows one to perceive the character of the coming Brazilian revolution.[89] He predicts that the subimperialist pact would tend to deepen, as the dominant classes moved to counter the inevitable response—the mass backlash to

---

84. Garcia and Sá, "Brazil," 388.
85. Marini, "Brazilian subimperialism."
86. Marini, "La dialéctica del desarrollo."
87. Garcia and Sá, "Brazil," 387.
88. Marini, "Memória," 75.
89. Marini, *Subdesarrollo*, 106–204.

dictatorship and super-exploitation—which was already happening on a continental scale and with revolutionary dimensions. "The union of the popular movements of Brazil and the rest of Latin America, that is to say the internationalization of the Latin American revolution, is thus the counterpart to the process of imperialist integration, inaugurated in its new phase by the Brazilian military coup."[90]

Marini's analysis of subimperialism and the Brazilian dictatorship resonated with intellectuals living under authoritarian regimes in the Southern Cone, namely in Argentina and Uruguay, fueling the clandestine Marxist debate on the phenomenon.[91] *Subdesarrollo y Revolución* enjoyed a wide readership throughout the 1970s, although by the following decade the author felt it to be somewhat out of date.[92] Marini's 1972 *Monthly Review* article—which he said was one of the few published texts in this period to examine the challenges of the revolutionary left from the inside—would be included as the final chapter of the volume's fifth edition, where he titled it, "Toward the Continental Revolution."[93] From the author's point of view, the book's positive reception was the result of three factors: the novelty of its concepts, which soon "crystallized in the theory of dependency"; its new methodology, "which sought to use Marxism in a creative way to build an understanding of the national process in Latin America"; and "its political audacity, which broke with the timorous and aseptic academicism that was the norm for studies of this nature."[94] Although not always with the author's permission, *Subdesarrollo y Revolución* was translated into French, Italian, and Portuguese, with an English edition planned by Penguin but abandoned for reasons Marini was never able to ascertain. Predictably, the dictatorship blocked its reception in Brazil, with entire shipments of the book being destroyed.[95]

---

90. Marini, "Brazilian interdependence," 29.
91. Marini, "Memória," 71–72.
92. Ibid., 82.
93. Marini, "Brazilian subimperialism."
94. Marini, "Memória," 82.
95. *Subdesarrollo y Revolución* would only be published in its entirety in Brazil in 2012, when it appeared as part of a series intending to recover the classic

## With the Student Movements of 1968

It is also in this period that Marini worked as a professor, and his relationship with his students and militants from the region's burgeoning student movements began to have an effect on his writing. Initially, he worked on synthesizing his approach to Latin American history and development—the approach he had begun to theorize during his time as a student in France. In 1966, he began to direct a course in international relations at UNAM, only to become vexed at the degree to which the existing curriculum, "suffer[ing] from an elitist paternalism," focused on developed countries.[96] Marini then turned to studying the region's development and history in a systematic way, combining global frameworks with country-specific studies, and placing specific foreign policy issues in their socioeconomic contexts.

In this period, Marini began to accompany the growing student movement in Brazil more attentively. Soon after his arrival to Mexico, he met Cláudio Colombani, an engineering student from São Paulo who impressed upon the author "how great the revolt against the reformism and accommodation of the PCB direction among young people was."[97] Marini would eventually meet a series of Brazilian student leaders recently released from prison for their activities against the dictatorship and granted asylum in Mexico. This group included Vladimir Palmeira, one of the leaders of the 1968 "March of One Hundred Thousand" aimed at the dictatorship. From these young people, Marini learned that his writings on the Brazilian coup were being circulated covertly by the Metropolitan Union of Students in Rio de Janeiro, a group that he had been affiliated with some years earlier.[98]

texts of critical Latin American thought, including Marxist dependency theory. This is the *Coleção Pátria Grande*, coordinated by Nildo Ouriques at the Institute of Latin American Studies (IELA) at the Universidade Federal de Santa Catarina. Ruy Mauro Marini, *Subdesenvolvimento e revolução*, trans. F. C. Prado and M. M. Gouvêa (Florianópolis, Brasil: Insular, 2012), https://iela.ufsc.br/colecao-patria-grande.

96. Marini, "Memória," 73–74.
97. Ibid., 68–69.
98. Ibid., 70–71, 80–81.

Meanwhile, Mexican workers and students were attempting to remake the very foundations of their country. Starting in the late 1950s, various groups of workers (teachers, oil workers, miners, electrical workers, and most notably railway workers) responded to the deep inequalities generated by a government policy known as "development stabilization" with a series of mass mobilizations, only to face a crackdown in 1959. Strikes diminished in the years that followed. Yet trade unions continued during the 1960s to campaign against contract violations and for the recognition of new unions, collective agreements, union democracy—all within state-controlled or corporatist union structures.[99]

During the same period, the student movement started to grow on university campuses, with calls for "the democratization of their centers of study, the expansion of their popular character, and university reform; and on the other hand, against the anti-popular administration of the state governments of Guerrero, Puebla, Michoacán, Sonora, and Tabasco."[100] A year and a half after Marini's arrival, students at UNAM would force the university rector, Ignacio Chávez Sánchez, to resign and the internal security forces to be removed from campus. In keeping with the increasingly autonomous forms of organization and ideological precision that characterized student movements elsewhere in the region at this time, Mexican students managed to wrest control of the student societies away from affiliates of the ruling party, the PRI.[101] They did so in response to state interference in the constitutionally guaranteed autonomy of the university.[102] By early 1968, in the midst of the "systematic and often brutal repression of mass movements, particularly of the working class," student organizations created new spaces of national convergence (e.g., the University Student Council and the National Central of Democratic Students), coming together

99. Max Ortega and Ana Alicia Solís de Alba, *La izquierda mexicana, una historia inacaba* (Mexico, D.F.: Editorial Itaca, 2012).
100. Ibid., 21–22.
101. Ruy Mauro Marini, "Os movimentos estudantis na América Latina," trans. Jonathan Jaumont, 1970, https://marini-escritos.unam.mx/?p=1272.
102. Keen and Haynes, *A History*, 336.

around calls for the democratization, not only of higher education, but of the political system and economy more generally.[103]

In an article surveying such movements in Latin America, Marini appeals to common structural factors and experiences in the region's educational systems to explain the rise of student militancy.[104] The article charts the explosion of student enrollment in education systems plagued by stagnating or falling investment; systems which, moreover, were poorly fitted to the development of the productive forces of the countries in question.[105] In the face of the student movement, the government's only response was to threaten privatization, spurred by funders such as USAID, BID, the OAS, the Pentagon, and private foundations. Marini interpreted this as "an attempt to disarticulate one of the best organized and most militant sectors of the population."[106] He accounted for the radicalization and increasingly mass character of the student movements, including the Mexican one, in this way:

> Students are slowly becoming aware of the fact that their university-level demands cannot find solutions in the economic setting in which they live and that, even if some demands were to be met, that would not solve their professional challenge. The struggle for structural change thus imposes itself as a necessity on the student and leads him to occupy the terrain of class struggle all the more firmly.[107]

Recognizing the need for deep social transformation, the Mexican student movement sought unity with urban workers, as a strategic imperative. "Student organization must necessarily conclude in popular organization that, by opposing the obstacles that hinder the historical development of Mexico, will make a reality out of our movement's slogan: Democratic Freedoms."[108] Student efforts to create a united

---

103. Marini, "Os movimentos," 9; Ortega and Solís de Alba, *La izquierda*, 23.
104. Marini, "Os movimentos."
105. Ibid., 5.
106. Ibid., 7.
107. Ibid., 11.
108. Consejo Nacional de Huelga, "Manifiesto a la nación '2 de octubre,'" in

front with workers based on these demands were met with silence from state-controlled union centrals. Still, the student movement grew and "gained a presence in the streets, in the factories and working-class neighbourhoods."[109] This, in turn, played a crucial role in mobilizing public opinion against the regime.[110] By August 1968, most UNAM schools and faculties, and the professors' union led by Félix Barro, had participated in coordinated nationwide actions with students from the National Polytechnic Institute (IPN), who were joined by workers from the National Railway Council, as well as groups of ceramic workers, oil workers, electrical workers, distance education workers, and public sector employees. The active participation of unions and union federations in the movement swelled over the following month, taking the form of "marches and student brigades, the formation of workers' struggle committees [comités de lucha], and some attempts to carry out solidarity work stoppages in workplaces."[111]

By 1968, Marini had joined CELA, invited there by Leopoldo Zea to deliver a course on Brazilian history. The course proved very popular, drawing leftist students from throughout the university, including leaders of the student movement. At their request, Marini delivered a seminar on the first volume of Marx's *Capital* at his home, which drew together students and younger faculty members from UNAM and the Colégio de México.[112] Because of the pressures they were under, some students joked that Marini might ultimately have to hold the seminar in prison. Beyond matters related to Marx's *Capital*, Marini also had informal conversations in this context with released Brazilian political prisoners, including Vladimir Palmeira, which led to his decision to bring together his writings on the Brazilian coup in *Subdesarrollo y Revolución* in his final months in Mexico. Marini received special encouragement from Cláudio Colombani in this project.

---

Ortega and Solís de Alba, *La izquierda*, 26.

109. Ortega and Solís de Alba, *La izquierda*, 24.

110. Marini, "Os movimentos," 9.

111. Ortega and Solís de Alba, *La izquierda*, 25.

112. Marini, "Memória," 77.

In May of the same year, Marini contributed an article to *El Día*, an establishment newspaper, on the tactics, organization, and program of the Brazilian popular movement. However, the article would only appear months later, in August, right after an upsurge in the student and popular movement that "shook the Mexican establishment to its foundations and became one of the most important points of rupture in the country's history."[113] From the perspective of Marini's own security, the timing was unfortunate. The author came under increasing pressure and surveillance, including wiretapping. In an attempt to resolve this situation, he set up a meeting with the Undersecretary of the Interior. The official suggested in no uncertain terms that foreign agitators—including Marini—had turned otherwise "good Mexican youth" against their own country. He hinted that Marini's leaving the country would be taken as a "sign of collaboration." Marini reluctantly began to contemplate a second exile. As pressure from the Mexican state ebbed and flowed over the following weeks, he could observe the collusion between the PRI government and the Brazilian dictatorship, to the degree that the former attempted to block the ability of already exiled Brazilian dissidents to congregate in yet another location.[114]

On the evening of October 2, 1968, the National Army opened fire on an unarmed student protest in the Plaza de las Tres Culturas, in the capital's Tlatelolco district. They did so on orders from President Gustavo Díaz Ordaz and Interior Minister Luís Echeverría. Over the course of the night, hundreds of youths, student leaders, and workers would be murdered or disappeared, and over a thousand arrested.[115] The event unleashed a wave of repression that signalled the escalation of the PRI's dirty war against popular resistance, backed solidly by the U.S. State Department.[116] The popular movement would carry on for

---

113. Ibid., 78.

114. Marini, "Memória," 79–80.

115. The precise number of people killed in this incident is still unknown. Keen and Haynes, *A History*, 336.

116. Kate Doyle, ed., *Tlatelolco Massacre: U.S. Documents on Mexico and the Events of 1968*, Electronic Briefing Book 99, National Security Archive, George Washington University, https://nsarchive2.gwu.edu/NSAEBB/NSAEBB99/.

an additional three months following the massacre. It then entered a
period of reflection in which militants decided that they needed to
expand the movement's reach and diversify its forms of struggle.

Following the massacre, Marini's situation in Mexico became unten-
able. Forced into exile for a second time, Marini was joining a New Left
that was preparing for another decade of struggle. A former student
would later describe the historical moment with these words:

> The student revolt of 1968 . . . really revolutionized relations between
> society and the political system and was a critical point in the cul-
> tural battle against the conservativism of certain countries of Latin
> America. From the student movement of 1968 emerged new ways of
> understanding and relating to politics, with culture and with knowl-
> edge, which provoked (and provokes) significant consequences then
> and now. The discussions with Ruy addressed all of this as a way
> to put the world puzzle back together again from a Latin American
> perspective, always with the idea that Latin America did not have a
> passive existence.[117]

117. Ceceña, "Ruy Mauro Marini," 292.

## SECOND EXILE: CHILE 1969-1973

*Yo pisaré las calles nuevamente*
*de lo que fue Santiago*
*ensangrentada*
*y en una hermosa plaza liberada*
*me detendré a llorar por los*
*ausentes.*

. . . . . .

*Retornarán los libros las canciones*
*que quemaron las manos asesinas*
*Renacerá mi pueblo de su ruina*
*y pagarán su culpa los traidores.*

I will walk the streets again
of what was bloody Santiago
and in a beautiful liberated square
I will stop to cry for the absent ones.

. . . . . .

Books will bring back the songs
that burned the murderous hands.
My people will be reborn from their
   ruin
and the traitors will pay for their guilt.

—From "Yo pisaré las calles nuevamente," written by Pablo Milanes in memory of Miguel Enríquez, founder of the MIR, killed by the Chilean secret police in 1974

Marini was forced to leave Mexico without official documents. It was Theotonio dos Santos and Vânia Bambirra who (appealing to the then-senator Salvador Allende) facilitated his entrance visa, and met him in the airport in November 1969.[118] A growing awareness of Marini's work among the Chilean left, notably among younger militants, helped him to settle into this new context. During his four short years in Chile, Marini would publish his most celebrated works and take part in a vibrant conversation in which the main contours of Marxist dependency theory unfolded. Marini was also able to test some of these ideas in practice, helping to define the revolutionary line in the most fervent debates of the day. Dos Santos later stated about this period:

We took these ideas abroad in search of a new theory of dependency. The theory of dependency was never an academic theory. It was a

118. Kay, "Theotonio dos Santos," 604; Vânia Bambirra, "Ruy Mauro Marini: meu melhor amigo!," in Traspadini and Stedile, *Ruy Mauro Marini—vida e obra*, 283–88.

political endeavor, an attempt to develop a noncommunist revolutionary theory.[119]

In March 1970, Marini took up residence in the old industrial city of Concepción, taking a position at the Central Institute of Sociology at the University of Concepción. Nelson Gutiérrez, a former student leader at the university, helped him obtain the position. Gutiérrez had been exposed to Marini's ideas through his contact with Brazilians in Santiago. He later commented, "I knew that the professor . . . would help me to resolve issues that concerned me daily, summed up in the phrase: without theory, no revolutionary action is possible."[120] For Marini, the decision to move to Concepción was an overtly political one: "If the level of politicization was high in Santiago [with the formation of the Unidad Popular coalition], it would acquire explosive connotations [in Concepción]."[121] In August 1965, the Revolutionary Left Movement (Movimiento de Izquierda Revolucionaria, or MIR) was created in Santiago, driven in large measure by young people at the University of Concepción. The group was established at a "Congress of Revolutionary Unity" that brought together members of the Revolutionary Marxist Vanguard, a youth federation that had been expelled from the Socialist Party a year earlier; several student organizations, including the Student Federation of the University of Concepción; trade unionists from the Central Unica de Trabajadores (CUT); the Agrupación Nacional de Empleados Fiscales (ANEF); and militants from a variety of ideological camps, including Trotskyists, dissident communists (some shaped by the Sino-Soviet split), dissident Christians, left-libertarians, and anarcho-syndicalists.[122] Despite its roots in a different conjuncture and setting, the MIR's

119. I assume that by "noncommunist," dos Santos means an alternative to the official communist parties of the day. Theotonio dos Santos in Chilcote, *Intellectuals*, 185.

120. Gutiérrez, "Ruy Mauro Marini," 264.

121. Marini, "Memória," 85.

122. Manuel Cabieses Donoso, "Aniversario del Movimiento de Izquierda Revolucionario (MIR): El honor y la rebeldía," *Rebelión.org*, August 16, 2018, https://rebelion.org/el-honor-y-la-rebeldia.

emergence responded to many of the same issues as those that had given rise to POLOP. The MIR also shared much of the latter's theoretical and strategic orientations. Its 1965 founding documents identify Chile as a semicolonial country, with an economy characterized by unequal and combined development, and with its most modern industrial sectors subordinated to imperialist interests. The MIR condemned the Chilean ruling class's inability, after 150 years of independence, to fulfill even the basic tasks of a democratic bourgeoisie, including national liberation, agrarian reform, and liquidating the holdovers from the country's semifeudal past. It concluded that the contradictions of the Chilean system would inevitably end in fascism ("Declaración de Princípios," September 1965). According to the MIR, the strategy of the traditional left, based on an attempt to reform the capitalist system through collaboration with the bourgeoisie and the search for a "peaceful path" to socialism, would only waste workers' hopes and energies. The tendency placed itself squarely in the socialist camp and found inspiration in the worldwide wave of revolutionary challenges to imperialism, even in countries supposedly without a "mature" proletariat. The MIR argued that the revolutionary process in Chile must reflect its unique class formation, and be built on an alliance between the "national majority [composed] of workers, peasants, and impoverished middle sectors" in the cities and countryside.[123]

The MIR's leadership initially included medical doctors Miguel Enríquez Espinosa and Bautista Van Schowen, and medical student Luciano Cruz (all of whom would be killed during the Pinochet assault or assassinated in its aftermath by the Chilean secret police). Later Nelson Gutiérrez became a MIR leader. Under increasing repression by the regime of Eduardo Frei Montalva (1964–70), the tendency broke with its Trotskyist members and redefined itself as an entirely Marxist-Leninist organization in 1967, with Miguel Enríquez as

---

123. See the "Declaración de Principios" (September 1965) and "Programa del Movimiento de Izquierda Revolucionario (MIR de Chile)" (August 15, 1965), both available at the Archivo MIR-Chile, hosted by the Centro Estudios Miguel Énriquez (CEME), https://www.archivochile.com/Archivo_Mir/Mir_libros_sobre/html/mir_archivo.html.

general secretary. In 1969, the MIR began to prepare students, the rural and urban poor, and the working classes for armed struggle.[124] This move led to a ban by the Frei regime and the capture and torture of several MIR leaders. In the end, the 1973 coup would cut short this fervent process of clandestine construction, after just five years.[125]

Marini joined the MIR soon after his arrival in Chile, and would remain one of its key intellectual drivers until the end of his life.[126] The group's social bases included several trade unions in Concepción and the surrounding region, whose work extended to the traditional coal mining communes (small cities) of Lota and Coronel, the historical birthplace of the Chilean Communist Party. In this setting, Marini worked with the MIR's political commission to shape its theoretical line and praxis, but also in the political formation of its cadres. Nelson Gutiérrez recalls:

> [Marini's] life had been transformed in such an intense way that it led him to an incessant pedagogical practice, both in classes and in meetings with militants and worker leaders from the coal mines of Lota, Coronel, and Arauco, the weavers of Tomé, the leather and shoe industry of Concepción, and with high school and university student leaders from the south of the country.[127]

It was in this context—with Marini shuttling between the university and clandestine work in Concepción—that his students and comrades began to call him the *maestro*, or sage.[128]

In September 1970, Marini relocated to Santiago to take a position as senior researcher at the Center of Socio-Economic Studies (CESO) at the University of Chile. He did so at the urging of dos Santos but also because of the political exigencies of the moment, defined by

124. Gutiérrez, "Ruy Mauro Marini," 266.
125. Cabieses, "Aniversario."
126. Gutiérrez, "Ruy Mauro Marini."
127. Gutiérrez, "Ruy Mauro Marini," 264.
128. Jaime Osorio, email exchange with author, July 4, 2021.

Allende's recent presidential victory.[129] From its founding in 1965 to its peak in 1972, CESO was a point of convergence for a generation of Marxist and left intellectuals, attracting people from throughout the region as well as from Europe and North America.[130] Here, Marini found community inside a "vast colony" of exiled Brazilians, among them dos Santos and Bambirra (who had arrived in mid-1966); Andre Gunder Frank and his wife, Marta Fuentes; and many members of the new Chilean left.[131] His colleagues included Tomás Vasconi, Marta Harnecker, Julio López Gallardo, as well as younger colleagues including Jaime Osorio (a student leader from the Faculty of Sociology), Orlando Caputo, Roberto Pizarro, Álvaro Briones, Antonio Sánchez, Guillermo Labarca, and Brazilians Marco Aurelio García and Emir Sader, among others. By this time, Maria da Conceição Tavares had joined CEPAL and Fernando Henrique Cardoso had entered the Latin American Institute of Economic and Social Planning (Instituto Latinoamericano de Planificación Económica y Social, ILPES) —both institutions having their headquarters in Santiago.[132]

According to Vânia Bambirra, the work at CESO represented the "most consistent effort to develop a 'Marxist theory of dependency.'"[133] In mid-1967, Theotonio dos Santos launched a project to examine dependency in particular national contexts, and in a 1968 report he produced one of the first definitions of "dependency" as such.[134] This project would, in turn, influence the program of the Unidad Popular (UP). Despite their rich collaboration in CESO, dos Santos, Bambirra, and Marini began to move in different directions politically at this

129. Kay, "Theotonio dos Santos," 604; Olave, "Ruy Mauro Marini," 13.

130. Marini, "Memória," 87–88; Kay, "Theotonio dos Santos," 614.

131. Marini, "Memória," 84–85.

132. Ibid.; Gutiérrez, "Ruy Mauro Marini," 267; Carla Ferreira, Jaime Osorio, and Mathias Luce, eds., *Padrão de reprodução do capital: contribuições da teoria marxista da dependência* (São Paulo: Boitempo Editorial, 2012), 9.

133. Kay, "Theotonio dos Santos," 139; see also Dal Rosso and Seabra, "A teoria marxista da dependência."

134. Kay, "Theotonio dos Santos," 605.

time.[135] Although all three critiqued the ideas coming out of CEPAL, the former two joined the UP coalition in an effort to influence its program (which dos Santos said was "a major stimulus to intellectual work, a fantastic laboratory for analyzing social change and revolution"), whereas the latter maintained a *mirista* (pro-MIR) position and a critical distance from the UP.[136]

## La Dialéctica de la Dependencia

In 1966, Ruy Mauro began to gather preliminary notes toward his seminal work, *Dialéctica de la dependencia*, in what would become known as his "red book" (in reality, a red folder). However, it was in the context of a 1971 seminar called "Marxist Theory and Latin American Reality" that the essay began to take shape. The seminar was part of a series in the dependent capitalism unit at CESO, which Marini directed. His plan was to

> begin with Marx's *Capital*. The seminar was to include Marx's political works, but, given [the 1973 coup], it did not go beyond the first part. It was not a simple reading of the book but rather—drawing on the Mexican experience—[an effort] to take it as a guiding thread for a discussion on how to apply its categories, principles, and laws to the study of Latin America.[137]

Judging from Marini's account of the period, we can surmise the role that dialogue with his students and colleagues—both in Chile and earlier in Mexico—played in the elaboration of the text.[138] Among his interlocuters in Chile were: Emir Sader, Andre Gunder Frank, Tomás Vasconi, Marco Aurelio Garcia, Cristián Sepúlveda, and Jaime Osorio.[139]

---

135. Ibid., 615.
136. Ibid., 610, 621.
137. Marini, "Memória," 89.
138. Marini, "Memória," 89–90.
139. Jaime Osorio, email exchange with author, September 26, 2021.

An early version of the text, featuring a historical orientation with which Marini was ultimately unsatisfied, was lost when his red book was destroyed in the "genocidal and incendiary fury" of a military raid on the first day of the coup: September 11, 1973.[140] Even prior to this, however, an incomplete version was published by CESO as a working paper in the first issue of its house journal, *Sociedad y Desarrollo,* in March 1972.[141] This version would appear as the introduction to an Italian translation of the book *Subdesarrollo y Revolución,* published by Einaudi in 1974.[142]

In its subsequent and complete form, the essay begins with a critique of the tendency of orthodox Marxists of the time to reduce all Third World social formations to the catchall abstraction of "precapitalism." The critique turns on Marini's observation that the Latin American colonial economy emerged in "tight consonance" with European capitalism and the nascent world system. Latin America's role was initially that of a producer of raw materials and precious metals, which made mercantile trade and banking in Europe possible.[143] By the mid-nineteenth century, its integration with the world market shifted to the primary export model (initially in Brazil and Chile, before becoming generalized in the region). In Marini's words, this model "appeared as the process and result of the transition to capitalism, and ... [was] the form that this capitalism assumed" in the periphery.[144] Taking issue with the scope of Andre Gunder Frank's study of the "development of underdevelopment," Marini stresses that dependency in this era is

140. Gutiérrez, "Ruy Mauro Marini," 268.

141. Ruy Mauro Marini, "Dialéctica de la dependencia: la economía exportadora," *Sociedad & Desarrollo* 1 (January–March 1972): 35–51, https://marini-escritos.unam.mx/wp-content/uploads/1991/01/3.3-Diale%CC%81ctica-de-la-dependencia.pdf. This early version is also interesting due to the inclusion of an English-language abstract on the final page.

142. Ruy Mauro Marini, *Il subimperialismo brasiliano* (Turin, Italy: Einaudi, 1974); Marini, "Memória," 90; Prado and Gouvêa, in Marini, *Subdesenvolvimento,* 25.

143. Ruy Mauro Marini, "Dialéctica de la dependencia," in *Dialéctica de la dependencia* (Mexico, D.F.: Ediciones Era, 1973), 16–19.

144. Marini, "Memória," 91.

not the same as the relations of subordination that developed under
the colonial or mercantile system.[145] He states that the challenge of his
theoretical task "is precisely in capturing this originality and, above
all, in discerning the moment in which originality implies a qualitative
change."[146]

To this end, Marini defines dependency as "a relation of subordination between formally independent nations, in the framework of which
the relations of production of the subordinate nations are modified or
re-created to ensure the expanded reproduction of dependency."[147]
Beginning with trade and circulation, he examines the unequal
exchange that tends to result from

> transactions between nations exchanging different kinds of com-
> modities, such as manufactures and raw materials—the mere fact
> that some produce goods that the rest do not, or that they cannot
> produce as easily, allows the former to evade the law of value; that is,
> to sell their products at prices higher than their value, thus giving rise
> to an unequal exchange.[148]

Over time, commodities of the dependent economy (primary products) are sold on the world market at prices lower than their value,
effecting a transfer of value from the dependent economy to the metropole when exchanged for the latter's more technologically advanced
manufactured goods. This, in turn, offsets the tendency of the rate of
profit in the metropole to fall, as a result of the increasing organic composition of capital there.[149]

Crucially, this exchange brings about a qualitative shift in the productive relations (in a word, *development*) of both the dependent

145. Andre Gunder Frank, "The Development of Underdevelopment," *Monthly
Review* 18, no. 4 (September 1966): 17–31.
146. Marini, "Dialéctica" (1973), 19.
147. Ibid., 18.
148. Ibid., 34.
149. Ibid., 27.

economy and of the metropole, but in highly divergent ways.[150] In the mid-nineteenth century, cheap raw materials acquired from Latin America fed the technologically improved labor processes in English industry, while cheap foodstuffs likewise lowered the cost of social reproduction for the English worker. In this way, the region contributed to the dramatic uptick in the productivity of the English working class, marking a shift of emphasis from accumulation centered on the production of absolute surplus value to that centered on relative surplus value. In this way, Latin America had a role in boosting the second wave of the Industrial Revolution (starting in the 1840s). However, to meet this heightened demand and compensate for the surplus value lost through unequal exchange, the Latin American oligarchy resorted not to a similar transformation of the technical bases of production but to super-exploitation of its labor power:

> We have seen that the problem that unequal exchange poses for Latin America is not precisely that of counteracting the transfer of value it implies, but rather that of compensating for a loss of surplus value; and that, unable to prevent this loss at the level of market relations,

---

150. And to varying degrees, given the matrix of likewise diverse exploitative relations between the British metropole and other parts of its formal and informal empire. It is interesting to note the degree to which Britain continued to rely on the products (foodstuffs and raw materials) of super-exploited labor from a social formation whose productive apparatus was still very much centered on racialized and enslaved labor (i.e., Brazil, where slavery would persist until 1888) at the very moment that it was vociferously declaring an end to its reliance on enslaved labor in its own Caribbean colonies. This mirrors what takes place in our time, when the great centers of outgoing investment (including from the still "green and pleasant lands" from where I write) claim to be standard bearers on issues of environmental and social justice while simultaneously outsourcing responsibility and blame for super-exploitation, poor and unhealthy working conditions, union busting, human rights violations, and environmental damage and greenhouse gas emissions along global production chains. Coming back to the period under study, the interconnections between differently exploited labor powers (including those subject to super-exploitation) at different nodal points of the imperialist division of labor of this period, have yet to be mapped.

the dependent economy reacts by compensating for it at the level of domestic production.[151]

This compensation occurs through various mechanisms associated with the production of relative and absolute surplus value, and often combinations thereof: increasing the intensity of labor through greater rates of exploitation, rather than developing workers' productive capacity; the prolongation of the working day, and specifically of surplus labor time; but also, crucially, by reducing the necessary consumption fund of the worker below its normal level, so that part of that fund also becomes a fund of accumulation.[152] This is Marini's definition of super-exploitation.

The metropole's demand for primary products, the value transfers it implies, and the super-exploitation that local bourgeoisies apply to make up for the loss, underpin the dominance of labor-intensive mono-production in the plantations and mines of Latin America, removing any incentive for developing the productive apparatus in a generalized way.[153] The reproduction of super-exploitation in successive periods hinders the transition from absolute to relative surplus value in underdeveloped countries, thereby reproducing the pattern of dependent capitalism.

In dependent nations, the option of resorting to super-exploitation also generates a second point of divergence from the economies of the metropole, this one in the circuit of capital. In England during the period under study, the circuit of capital reinforces and in fact enables the integrity of the nation-state (notwithstanding its transnational existence as an imperialist state). However, in dependent economies, this integrity is obstructed insofar as commodities are continually sold to the outside world, something that can be sustained so long as a "sufficiently large surplus population exists."[154] In other words, whereas

---

151. Ibid., 38.

152. Ibid., 38–40.

153. Marini, "Memória," 91.

154. Kay, *Latin American Theories*, 146. On the surface, this resonates with CEPAL's thesis on structural dualism, described by Garcia and Sá: "[Dualism]

English workers were paid enough to consume some of the very use values they produced without sacrificing the rate of profit, in Latin America, the functions of worker and consumer are pulled apart. Working-class consumption becomes so limited that the worker is not able to aid in the realization of capital investment, which occurs instead through external markets. Hence, even when it occurs, "industrialization does not fundamentally alter the model of capital accumulation in Latin America, which continues to rely on the over-exploitation of labour."[155]

Marini next draws conclusions that are as audacious as his analysis. He argues that the characteristics of the dependent economy, diverging from those of the metropole, are nonetheless equally germane to the capitalist mode of production, in that "underdevelopment is the other face of development."[156] In his view, this kind of "capitalism *sui generis*," as a mode of production, only makes sense if one considers the system as a whole, as much at the national as at the international level.[157] It follows from Marini's arguments that greater engagement

---

... refers to a notion according to which a great heterogeneity in the productive apparatus would give rise to 'two worlds' and 'historical times' coexisting simultaneously—the modernized elite, on the one hand, and the backward masses, especially the rural ones, on the other, without, however, merging into an integrated market, nor indeed constituting *one* society proper. The closure of this social gap—the major goal of [CEPAL] development policies—would ultimately depend on a broad reform of the world economy as a whole that would end the core-periphery structure, and thus enable capitalism to flourish in countries, such as Brazil, that were historically underprivileged by the international division of labour." Garcia and Sá, "Brazil," 387. Marini's work problematizes the CEPAL thesis by showing the imbrication of the so-called backward agrarian structure and more advanced industries, i.e. the degree to which the former is connected with the more dynamic sectors of industry. "Backward agrarian structures" in Brazil's interior continue to fulfill this role even today.

155. Ibid. Kay opts for the word *over-exploitation* in his translation of *super-explotación*. In our view, *super-exploitation* is more accurate.
156. Marini, "Memória," 90; Jaime Osorio, "Dialectics, Super-exploitation, and Dependency," in this volume, 171.
157. Marini, "Dialéctica" (1973), 14.

with this international division of labor will only deepen dependency, if the productive relations underpinning it are not destroyed.[158]

## The Marini-Cardoso Debate

The publication of *Dialéctica de la dependencia* marked the beginning of a period in which Marini's ideas began to attract critical engagement, both in the form of deep study and attacks.[159] The most notorious critique came from Fernando Henrique Cardoso, who made a first intervention in 1972 and a second one, with José Serra, in 1978.[160] Marini responded to their arguments and certain misconceptions in a series of texts, which helped to articulate more sharply his thesis on dependency as a particular form of capitalist development and his arguments regarding super-exploitation.[161] The debate between Cardoso and Marini reflects key tensions between the Marxist and structuralist

---

158. Ibid., 18. In the final chapter of this volume, Jaime Osorio addresses the context in which *Dialéctica de la dependencia* first appeared. He also deals in depth with the implications of Marini's thesis both for Marxist theory and political strategies in the region.

159. Marini, "Memória," 132.

160. Fernando Henrique Cardoso, "Notas sobre el estado actual de los estúdios sobre dependência" (Santiago, Chile: Instituto Latinoamericana de Planificación Económica y Social, CEPAL, 1974), https://repositorio.cepal. org/handle/11362/34470 (originally published in *Revista Latinoamericana de Ciencias Sociales* 4 (1972); José Serra and Fernando Henrique Cardoso, "Las desventuras de la dialéctica de la dependencia," *Revista Mexicana de Sociología* 40 (Número extraordinario, 1978): 9–55; Cardoso and Faletto, *Dependency and Development*, originally published in Spanish in 1971. The most in-depth treatment of the debate in English can be found in chapter 6 of Kay's *Latin American Theories*, but see Prado's work for the way in which the debate was shaped and manipulated by Cardoso in Brazilian institutions to create a *pensée unique* surrounding dependency. Kay, *Latin American Theories*, 163–96; Prado, "Por qué hubo que desconocer."

161. Marini, "En torno a *Dialéctica*"; Marini, *Subdesarrollo*; Ruy Mauro Marini, "Las razones del neodesarrollismo (respuesta a F. H. Cardoso & J. Serra)," *Revista Mexicana de Sociología* 40 (Número extraordinario, 1978), 57–106. See Marini's "Memória" for the author's last word on the subject. Marini, "Memória," 92.

approaches to dependency and the question of what kind of development is possible in Latin America. Equally important in this period were the diverging implications of each position for political strategy.[162]

Cardoso's initial critique of *Dialéctica de la dependencia*, in 1972, coincided with the development of his own model of "associated dependent development." That model appealed to the main agents of the "tripod" structure that had fostered Brazilian industrialization since the Kubitschek administration of the late 1950s: state enterprises, multinational corporations, and the local businesses associated with each.[163] Cardoso takes issue with the supposed novelty of the concept of dependency, and rejects the idea that the search for "intermediate relations and articulations" represents a methodological advance in the theorization of dependent development.[164] More generally, he rejects any effort to arrive at a general theory or "law of dependency," given the degree to which dependency relies upon social relations that are by definition contingent.[165] Cardoso attempts to focus on these contingent structures of dependency, which can be overcome to allow for a degree of capital accumulation by local bourgeoisies, even as realization relies on foreign markets and luxury consumption by the same class.

Cardoso and Serra's 1978 essay takes more extensive aim at the terms of Marini's thesis on dependency, super-exploitation, and subimperialism. They begin by challenging Marini's formulation of unequal exchange and his suggestion that deteriorating terms of trade in favor of advanced economies will necessarily lead to a fall in the rate of profit in the periphery, leading local bourgeoisies to compensate for it by recurring to super-exploitation.[166] They likewise dismiss the author's intermediate category of subimperialism, which they suggest is not the necessary result of problems of capital realization (i.e., the inability to sell commodities and realize their value due to a limited domestic

---

162. Kay, *Latin American Theories*, 127.

163. Cardoso, "Notas," 31.

164. Cardoso in Chilcote, *Intellectuals*, 201–2.

165. Cardoso developed this point later with Enzo Faletto. Cardoso and Faletto, *Dependency and Development*.

166. Serra and Cardoso, "Las desventuras," 22–26.

market). Bizarrely, they try to make their case with data drawn precisely
from the period of intensified dictatorship, 1969 to 1975, which saw
the increased consumption of durable consumer goods by the middle
and upper classes, and of capital goods by the public sector and military government, rather than the masses.[167] Moving on to their main
objection, Serra and Cardoso argue that Marini has overstated the significance of labor super-exploitation, and underplayed the importance
of relative surplus value in dependent capitalist accumulation.[168] He
does so, they allege, by ignoring the role that technological advances
have played in lowering the cost of constant capital and raising labor
productivity (and so, the rate of profit), both in the historical development of capitalism and in the sectors producing durable consumer
goods dominated by monopoly capital in Brazil under the tripod
system. In this framework, industrialization on the footing established
by advanced economies *is* possible in a dependent country like Brazil.
Moreover, on the eve of a controlled return to democracy, the political
possibilities in Brazil extend well beyond Marini's binary of absolute
repression (fascism) or socialism, an analysis they allege to be based in
economism.[169]

Marini initially responded to Cardoso's critiques in his 1973 postscript, *En torno a Dialéctica de la dependencia* (included in this book),
as well as in the 1974 preface to the fifth edition of *Subdesarrollo y
Revolución*.[170] The former text was initially intended as a preface to the
book-length version of *Dialéctica*. However, as the author explains in
its first lines, he found it difficult to introduce an essay that was itself an
introduction to a new research agenda and to the conclusions he had
reached to date.[171] Later on, in his 1990 memoir, Marini also reflected
on the debate.[172] There, he notes that Cardoso's earliest response to
*Dialéctica* was based on the initial article issued by CESO, an

---

167. Ibid., 36–39.
168. Ibid., 42–45.
169. Ibid., 53.
170. Marini, "En torno a *Dialéctica*"; Marini, *Subdesarrollo*.
171. Marini, "En torno a *Dialéctica*," 81.
172. Marini, "Memória," 92, 118–19, 131, 133.

incomplete version that did not include his analysis of the industrialization process.[173] This, in turn, led to a series of misinterpretations of
Marini's arguments, which would be reproduced time and again, not
least of which by Cardoso himself.

Much of Marini's rebuttal involves a tacit defense of his apparent
points of departure from standard interpretations of Marx's theory of
capitalist development and the labor theory of value. These standard
interpretations involve universalizing assumptions that Cardoso and
his co-authors reproduce by insisting that capitalism operates and
unfolds everywhere in much the same manner as it did in advanced
economies. In part, Marini defends his analysis by challenging Cardoso
on the question of which phenomena—for example, the contradictory
reproduction of older modalities of exploitation and the expansion of
the relative surplus population even in times of growth—are actually
essential to the capitalist mode of production as it develops on a global
scale.[174] Further, he defends his use of Marx's own methodology, even
when challenging Marxist orthodoxy in the process.[175] Osorio argues
that for Marini

> it was necessary to re-create Marxism, but not to repeat Marx,
> because the unprecedented problem was to substantiate the exis-
> tence of a new modality of capitalism and to define its developmental
> trends within the framework of this relationship with the capitalist
> world system. That is what Marini's book, *Dialéctica de la dependen-
> cia*, offers to theory and Marxism. No more, and no less.[176]

---

173. Marini, "Dialéctica" (1972); Cardoso, "Notas"; Marini, "Memória," 92.
174. Marini, *Dialéctica de la dependencia* (1973), 91–95.
175. See Andy Higginbottom, "Structure and Essence in *Capital I*: extra surplus-
value and the stages of capitalism," *Journal of Australian Political Economy* 70
(Summer 2012): 251–70; Andy Higginbottom, "Superexplotación y *El Capital*:
entre el capitalismo actual globalizado y la plusvalía," in *Marxismos y Resistencias
en el Sur Global*, ed. N. Kohan and N. López (Madrid: AKAL, 2022).
176. Osorio, "Dialectics, Super-exploitation, and Dependency," in this volume,
172.

For this reason, in the 1973 postscript to *Dialéctica*, Marini clarifies the extent to which he adopted Marx's dialectical methodology used in the three volumes of *Capital*.[177] He cites Marx's caveat, "In theory, we assume that the laws of the capitalist mode of production develop in their pure form. In reality, this is only an approximation," before reminding us that his objective in the original essay was to attempt to "determine the *specific laws* by which the dependent economy is governed" in Latin America, which evolved "in the broader context of the laws of development of the system as a whole."[178]

Marini also responds to Cardoso's attempt to question the connection between unequal exchange and super-exploitation.[179] He defends his decision to start with circulation and the insertion of the Latin American economy in the world system, which mirrors the way Marx begins *Capital*, volume 1. He then shows how—in a world system composed of productive forces that vary significantly in terms of "their respective organic compositions of capital, which point to different forms and degrees of labor exploitation"—the heightened demand for food and raw materials by industrialized countries, whose economies are characterized by higher organic composition, will be met by the more extensive and intensive use of labor power in dependent ones. This causes "the value of the commodities produced [to increase], which makes surplus value and profit rise simultaneously."[180] The growth of Latin American exports in this period (until the 1870s) in turn drives direct investment from the metropole. Then, in the last quarter of the nineteenth century, the transfer of profits and surplus value

> to the industrial countries points toward the formation of an average rate of profit at the international level, which frees exchange from its strict dependence on the value of commodities. In other words, the importance that value had in the previous stage as the regulator of international transactions gradually gives way to the primacy of the

---

177. Marini, "En torno a *Dialéctica*."
178. Ibid., 82, 99.
179. Cardoso, "Notas"; Serra and Cardoso, "Las desventuras."
180. Marini, "En torno a *Dialéctica*," 87, 88.

price of production (the cost of production plus the average profit, which, as we have seen, is lower than surplus value in the case of dependent countries).[181]

Later, in his 1978 response to Cardoso and Serra, Marini would point out how he adopted Marx's conceptualization of prices of production in volume 3 of *Capital,* extending and modifying it to work at the *international* intersection of capitalist commodity production and circulation. [182] He argues that Cardoso and Serra have misunderstood the dialectical relation between prices and value as they operate at the international level:

> The only thing that circulation can do is to *compare* the socially necessary labor time for the production of commodities, that is, to compare their values; on this basis, the commercial price of each is determined, that is, a *relation of prices* is established between them, which, however much it may vary as a result of supply and/ or demand, *revolves around the comparison of values.* . . . The only effect that can be derived from the international mobility of labor power has to do with the *prices of production,* by favoring, on that plane, the formation of an average profit.[183]

The formation of international market prices allows for a transfer of value from Latin America to Europe and an unequal exchange of different socially necessary labor times. For this reason, Marini's critics have failed to recognize the significance of value-transfer mechanisms that exist (again, embedded in the normal functioning of the market) and which make it necessary for the subordinated bourgeoisies—particularly in the agriculture and mining sectors—to resort to super-exploitation.

Marini believed that the most damaging error made by Cardoso in

---

181. Ibid., 90.
182. Karl Marx, *Capital,* vol. 3, trans. David Fernbach (London: Penguin Books, 1991).
183. Marini, "Las razones," 64–65.

his 1972 essay was the conflation of super-exploitation with absolute
surplus value.[184] To this end, in the 1973 postscript, Marini attempts
to clarify the notion of super-exploitation by referring to his original
outline of the concept, which includes two elements that Cardoso
omitted: that super-exploitation may involve greater intensification of
labor, and that it necessarily

> affects the two labor times within the working day and not only sur-
> plus labor time, as is the case with absolute surplus value. For all
> these reasons, super-exploitation is defined more precisely by the
> greater exploitation of the worker's physical strength, as opposed to
> the exploitation resulting from increasing his productivity, and tends
> normally to be expressed in the fact that labor power is remunerated
> below its real value.[185]

Cardoso also mischaracterizes Marini's argument regarding relative
surplus value, suggesting it denies the possibility of increases to labor
productivity in dependent economies.[186] Marini's response is that the
task is rather to understand the character that relative surplus value
takes in these economies.[187] In *Dialéctica*, he did this by examining
"the tendency of the dependent economy to block the transfer of productivity gains to prices, fixing as extraordinary surplus value what
could become relative surplus value."[188] It is also a matter of determining the significance of all higher forms of exploitation in a given
dependent social formation as a whole:

> . . . what my essay intended to demonstrate is, first, that *capitalist pro-*
> *duction, by developing labor's productive powers, does not eliminate*

---

184. Marini, "En torno a *Dialéctica*"; Cardoso, "Notas," 28, 32; Marini,
"Memória," 92; see also Luce, *Teoria*, 135–96.
185. Marini, "En torno a *Dialéctica*," 92–93.
186. Cardoso, "Notas"; Serra and Cardoso, "Las desventuras"; Marini,
"Memória," 93.
187. Marini, "En torno a *Dialéctica*," 100.
188. Marini, "Memória," 93.

*but rather accentuates the greater exploitation of the worker;* and
second, that combinations of forms of capitalist exploitation are carried out in an unequal manner in the system as a whole, giving rise to
distinct social formations according to the predominance of a given
form.... the greater or lesser occurrence of the forms of exploitation
and their specific configuration *qualitatively modify the ways that the
system's laws of movement operate*, in particular the general law of
capital accumulation.[189]

In a statement that speaks to what are clearly ontological divergences
with Cardoso, Marini argues:

super-exploitation does not correspond to a survival of primitive
modes of capital accumulation, but *is something inherent to the latter
that grows in correlation with the development of the productive power
of labor.* To assume the opposite amounts to accepting that capitalism, to the degree that it approaches its pure ideal, becomes an
increasingly less *exploitative* system ...[190]

Brazilian history tends to confirm Marini's claims. In his later response
to Serra and Cardoso, he would point to how super-exploitation had

---

189. Italics in original. Marini, "En torno a *Dialéctica*," 93, 98.
190. Italics in original. Ibid., 98. In this passage, Marini is taking issue with the
"marginal mass" thesis of the 1970s. However, his comments may also appear to
resonate with Trotsky's observations on "uneven and combined development."
Regarding the relevance of Trotsky's thesis for Marxist dependency theorists,
including Marini, I agree with Mathias Luce's judgment: "However, we understand the latter [uneven and combined development] to be on a more general level
of abstraction, considering the unequal pace in the historical process for a wide
range of events. In contrast, the uneven development examined by MDT [inspired
by Lenin] is based primarily on the historical unfolding of the law of value and
on the differentiation of social-economic formations, in the context of the formation of the world market and the integration of productive systems, giving rise to
specific historical phenomena. This gives rise to tendential laws specific to the
dependent economy, originally discovered by MDT, and which are a sharpened
expression of capital's general laws." Luce, *Teoria*, 11n3, emphasis in the original.

increased under the Brazilian dictatorship. This was achieved with the suppression of trade unions and political repression, the explosion of the industrial reserve army, and the enforced suppression of real wages by the regime. Within the labor process itself, Brazilian workers saw the lengthening of the workday and the intensification of labor, which Serra and Cardoso neglect to mention as a concrete phenomenon.[191] Rather, in their view, Marini suggests, "The working class itself is to blame for the fact that its skin is being torn off its back."[192]

Coming back to Cardoso's thesis, what is clear in this exchange is the bourgeois position of the theorist and his co-author. This can be seen in the very definition of "associated dependent development" which they reduce to local accumulation—where "the national bourgeoisie and foreign capital were compatible and dependency and development no longer antagonistic"—while turning a blind eye to the forms and degrees of the working-class exploitation that made it possible.[193] Marini would refer to this somewhat mischievously in his memoir, stating that he originally thought to call his response to Cardoso and Serra "Why I am proud of my bourgeoisie." [194] He would also forcefully condemn Cardoso as an apologist for the dictatorship who conflated a violent model of accumulation installed by the military regime with the Brazilian bourgeois revolution.[195]

There are several interesting points to be made about what occurred in the wake of the debate. The first concerns the unequal reception and diffusion of the two positions. Tellingly, neither Marini's original text nor his later responses to Cardoso and Serra would be published

---

191. Marini, "Las razones," 95–98.

192. Ibid., 98. In this overview, I have omitted other elements of Marini's response in this debate, namely those related to subimperialism and the nature of the state. Please see Kay's *Latin American Theories*, which does justice to these themes. Kay, *Latin American Theories*, 168–69.

193. By contrast to the work of Marini, Bambirra, and dos Santos. Pablo Rieznik in Chilcote, *Intellectuals*, 200.

194. Marini, "Las razones."

195. Marini, *Subdesarrollo*, viii.

in Brazil until decades later.[196] By contrast, Cardoso and Serra successfully institutionalized their reformist position in Brazilian political sociology at the prestigious Centro Brasileiro de Análise e Planejamento (Cebrap) research unit in São Paulo, of which Cardoso was a cofounder, and which operated as an intellectual space for the democratic opposition to the dictatorship.[197] Fernando Correa Prado describes the precise ways in which Cardoso's line came to form a *pensée unique,* shaping how generations of students and militants would understand the debate around Latin American dependency theory. This was a line that openly asserted and then reproduced misrepresentations and even falsehoods regarding the Marxist strand of dependency theory of Marini, Frank, and dos Santos.[198] Unfortunately, these misrepresentations would go unanswered and uncorrected in the intellectual vacuum of Brazil during their exile.[199] Prado writes:

> Cardoso's views on the Marxist side of dependency theory, although untenable, were repeated in universities and, what is even worse, in centers of political formation. This process of establishing a "single line of thought" about the dependency controversy also involved the contribution of several important intellectuals, giving rise to a

---

196. Of Marini's contributions to this debate, only his final monograph would be published promptly after its completion in Brazil. Ruy Mauro Marini, *América Latina: Dependência e integração* (São Paulo: Editora Página Aberta, 1992); see also Ouriques, "Apresentação"; Prado, "Por qué hubo que desconocer."

197. Chilcote, *Intellectuals,* 157–62.

198. Prado observes that Cardoso's attacks on MDT left out the only woman among the tendency's founders, Vânia Bambirra, who was very much part of this debate. Kay, "Theotonio dos Santos"; Prado, "Por qué hubo que desconocer," 128n2. An online archive of Bambirra's work (including her efforts to include gender in the analysis of dependency) is maintained by the Laboratório de Estudos sobre Marx e a Teoria Marxista da Dependência (Laboratory of Studies on Marx and the Marxist Theory of Dependency, Lemarx-TMD/ESS) at the Federal University of Rio de Janeiro and the Research Unit in History at the Federal University of Rio Grande do Sul. Memorial-Arquivo Vania Bambirra, https://vaniabambirra. wordpress.com/, https://www.ufrgs.br/vaniabambirra.

199. Prado, "Por qué hubo que desconocer."

genuine "intellectual inertia" that has started to be broken in recent years.[200]

Whereas Marini's seminal essay is only now being published in English, Cardoso's responses to it and the elaboration of his Weberian approach to dependency would be published in English soon after their original publication, becoming one of the main touchstones in the conversation surrounding dependency in the English-speaking parts of the Global North.[201] In the United States, several pieces of Marini's conjunctural analysis would appear in publications such as *Monthly Review*, *Contemporary Marxism* (now *Social Justice*), *NACLA's Report on the Americas*, and *Latin American Perspectives* (whose editorial board included Marini). However, an English-language version of his theoretical masterwork never materialized.[202] In line with Prado and Ourique's claim that there was a *de facto* boycott of Marini's work in Brazil, I would argue that the lack of access to his work in English has limited the scope of debate surrounding dependency to its reformist and structuralist strands, which made it easier to discount dependency theory in the early years of neoliberalism.[203]

---

200. Ibid., 135.
201. For example, Fernando Henrique Cardoso, "The Consumption of Dependency Theory in the United States," *Latin American Research Review* 12, no. 3 (1977): 7–24; Cardoso and Faletto, *Dependency and Development*.
202. Marini, "Memória," 93; Chilcote, *Intellectuals*, 203.
203. Chilcote, *Intellectuals*, 200–201. See also Weeks and Dore's 1979 critique of the dependency thesis, in which they ignore much of the complexity of Marini's framework (e.g., the significance of internal class relations, the movement from circulation to production) only to charge him with being an underconsumptionist. They rely on Lenin and Bukharin's response to the Narodnik underconsumptionism thesis, arguing that "there is, in fact, no 'realization problem' (problem in converting surplus value into profit) since most of the realization of value occurs not through workers' (or even capitalists') consumption . . . but through the productive consumption of the means of production." John Weeks and Elizabeth Dore, "International exchange and the causes of backwardness," *Latin American Perspectives* 6, no. 2 (1979): 69–70. Despite their critique of Cardoso's "eclecticism," this part of their argument echoes Cardoso's claim that Brazilian workers

A second interesting point concerns the political trajectories of Marini's interlocutors following the debate. Both Cardoso and Serra came to distance themselves from any previous association with Marxism as they became key figures in Brazil's shift to neoliberalism following the end of the dictatorship. [204] Cardoso became Finance Minister under Itamar Franco (1992–94) and then President (1994–2002). Serra would enjoy several cabinet roles in Cardoso's administrations and become governor of the state of São Paulo (2007–2010). Both were members of the Brazilian Social Democracy Party (PSDB). Cardoso's misreading of Marini's theoretical argument in *Dialéctica* was openly brandished in Brazil's neoliberal period, with Cardoso reviving his own version of dependency theory during his first presidential mandate to justify the introduction of neoliberal reforms.[205] In 1996, he argued that the trade liberalization and privatizations slated in this package would permit the modernization of the technical bases of production and increase productivity, which this ex-Marxist boldly argued would signal the shift from absolute to relative surplus value. What was actually unleashed, however, was a new cycle of the general law of accumulation involving the displacement of millions of workers from the formal labor process and heightened rates of exploitation (including super-exploitation) for those who remained employed. Old errors die hard, especially when one is in power and under no compulsion to account for them.

Coming back to Marini's *Dialéctica de la dependencia*, even the incomplete version of the essay was warmly received and inspired many students. This prompted Marini to complete the work and see it published. It was first issued in 1973, by the Mexican publishing house Era, in a volume that included the author's first response to Cardoso.

---

as consumers mattered less to accumulation than the state's increased consumption of capital goods and durable consumer goods. See Serra and Cardoso, "Las desventuras," 36–39.

204. See Chilcote, *Intellectuals*, 141, 141n7.

205. Gustavo Codas, "Mais-valia e modernidade em FHC," *Boletim Quinzena*, Centro de Pastoral Vergueiro, no. 240 (1996): 14–17; see also Luiz Carlos Bresser-Pereira in Chilcote, *Intellectuals*, 200.

Over the next few years, despite Marini's doubts about publishing an essay reflecting an ongoing line of inquiry, *Dialéctica* would see several authorized editions (two Portuguese versions, in 1976 and 1981, as well as a German version in 1974 and a Dutch one in 1976) and various unauthorized editions (in France, Argentina, Spain, and Portugal).[206] In this period, the work "went on to be discussed, questioned and—almost always passionately and even in bad faith—attacked." However, Marini emphasized that he "did not live through this experience alone, which took place in the context of the critique of dependency theory which began in 1974."[207]

## Debating Unidad Popular

Marini's political work in the MIR took him throughout Chile. Meanwhile, he began to play an active role in the debate taking shape between the MIR, on the one hand, and the new government of Salvador Allende and the Unidad Popular coalition, on the other. This debate occurred as much within the space of CESO as within the MIR itself. He participated in the founding of a weekly magazine, *Chile Hoy*, with other members of CESO including dos Santos, Pío García, and Marta Harnecker, who would become its director and most frequent contributor. The aim of the magazine, which could readily be found at newspaper kiosks, was to investigate the roots of the opposition between the two projects—both ostensibly geared toward achieving socialism and overcoming dependency—with the goal of achieving greater unity in the Chilean left.[208] Marini directed the editorial board of a second, more substantive quarterly journal, *Marxismo y Revolución*, whose sub-director was also a colleague from CESO, Guillermo Labarca. Only one edition of the quarterly journal would see the light of day, being published just weeks prior to the military coup. Marini himself contributed conjunctural analyses to the journal, two of which would be included in the book *El reformismo y la contrarrevolución: Estudios*

---

206. Marini, "Memória," 93, 105.

207. Ibid., 132.

208. Ibid., 94.

*sobre Chile* (Reformism and Counterrevolution: Studies on Chile).[209]
Finally, Marini contributed to the main newspaper of the MIR, *El Rebelde*, which was started in the late 1960s. Both it and another key publication, *Punto Final*, could be purchased at neighborhood kiosks. With such publications, the MIR managed to project itself into the mass media and national debate, while attracting critical intellectuals and cultural workers from Chile and other countries inspired by the Chilean experience, who were "living through the revolution" and generating the "revolutionary self-awareness" it demanded.[210]

In "El desarrollo industrial dependiente y la crisis del sistema de dominación," an essay published in *Marxismo y Revolución* soon after the UP's electoral victory in November 1970, Marini criticizes the strategy underlying "the Chilean road to socialism" proposed by the coalition, which he characterizes as attempting to attract or neutralize key strata of the petty bourgeoisie.[211] His critique involves contextualizing the UP's strategy in the recent history of Chile's industrial development and rejecting the argument that the strategy of national development based on import-substituting industrialization has been "exhausted." This argument, he suggests, misses key dynamics of the previous decade: specifically, that industrial production has been increasingly divorced from the masses' consumption needs in favor of luxury consumption geared toward the highest levels of society, and the production of the intermediate goods that facilitate such consumption.

Along with these developments, there was a high degree of *concentration* and later *monopolization* in the more dynamic industrial

209. Ruy Mauro Marini, *El reformismo y la contrarrevolución: Estudios sobre Chile* (Mexico, D.F.: Ediciones Era, 1976), https://marini-escritos.unam.mx/?p=3165.
210. Ivette Lozoya López, *Científicos sociales latinoamericanos en el MIR chileno (1965–1973)* (Santiago, Chile: Ariadna Ediciones, 2020), https://books.openedition.org/ariadnaediciones/7622; Gutiérrez, "Ruy Mauro Marini," 269. Many thanks to Cristóbal Kay for his help with this section.
211. Marini, "El desarrollo industrial dependiente y la crisis del sistema de dominación," in *El reformismo y la contrarrevolución*, 55–85, https://marini-escritos.unam.mx/?p=1188.

sectors. Marini distinguishes between the former, "characterized by the expansion of a given capital, based on its own expanded reproduction," which is typical of periods of expansion, and the latter, a process of "centralization in which a given capital absorbs other already formed capitals," which is typical of periods with declining growth. In Chile, foreign investors played a role in the monopolization of industry in the postwar period, their presence having grown rapidly from 1960 to 1967, largely through FDI and shareholder participation. In the main, however, the process was carried out by the largest firms; the latter (whether national or foreign) were able to monopolize not only a given market, but also access to credit, and more important, to dominate the distribution of surplus value. Such firms tended to rely on advanced technology, but they also increased rates of exploitation in the labor process, generating extraordinary rates of surplus value and profit. Marini argues that a strategy that downplays the role of industrial workers and invests instead in a layer of the petty bourgeoisie will only aggravate the political crisis. The petty bourgeoisie—owners of small and medium enterprises squeezed out by the process of monopolization—may in the last instance revert to a defense of the bourgeois state. Arguably, Marini's analysis proved to be correct.

Marini would later say that his time in Chile "corresponded to . . . my arrival to maturity both on an intellectual and political level."[212] On the first day of the coup, there was a raid on Marini's small apartment in Providencia, a place where *miristas*, exiles, and friends had taken to gathering.[213] The author took refuge in the Panamanian embassy with several friends.

The events that marked [the end of exile]—the military coup of September 11, the experience of state terrorism to its highest degree, the days passed in the Panamanian embassy, where close to 200 people made a disciplined and supportive (*solidario*) effort to co-exist in a small apartment, under the noise of bombs and

---

212. Marini, "Memória," 99.
213. Gutiérrez, "Ruy Mauro Marini," 270.

gunfire—were experienced naturally, as contingencies of a process whose historical significance was perfectly clear to me.[214]

With rumors flying that he had been among the thousands imprisoned in the Estadio Nacional (and perhaps, even executed), Marini was forced to flee—once more, with few possessions. He spoke warmly of the solidarity shown by friends and comrades, including that of his housecleaner, who managed to locate some money. "This was one of the more moving manifestations of solidarity that I received then, on the part of Chileans who were humble, the most conscious and combative."[215] The author left for Panama in mid-October, where he remained until January 1974.

## THIRD EXILE: MEXICO 1974–1984

| | |
|---|---|
| *Pero no cambia mi amor* | But it does not change my love |
| *Por más lejos que me encuentre* | No matter how far away I may be, |
| *Ni el recuerdo, ni el dolor* | Neither the memory, nor the pain |
| *De mi pueblo y de gente* | Of my home and people |
| | |
| *Lo que cambió ayer* | That which changed yesterday |
| *Tendrá que cambiar mañana* | Will have to change tomorrow |
| *Así como cambio yo* | Just as I keep changing |
| *En esta tierra lejana* | In this distant land |

—From "Todo Cambia," lyrics by Julio Numhauser, performed by Mercedes Sosa

Over the next few months, there were efforts to help Marini relocate, and he received several offers of work. Marini wanted to settle in Argentina, because of its proximity to Chile, or return to Mexico, "for sentimental reasons."[216] However, the MIR's political commission requested that

---

214. Marini, "Memória," 99.
215. Ibid., 100.
216. Ibid., 100–101.

he relocate to Europe, home of the largest solidarity movement with the Chilean people outside of Latin America—a political network built partly through personal connections fostered at CESO.[217] At the outset of 1974, Marini moved to Munich to join the Max Planck Institute. He did so on the invitation of Otto Kreye, whom he had met earlier in the year at a conference organized by Samir Amin. In Munich, he was able to reconnect with former colleagues from CESO, including Antonio Sánchez, Marcelo García, and Andre Gunder Frank. However, Marini took on a post as visiting professor at the Center of Latin American Studies at UNAM in September of the same year, allowing him to return to Mexico City. He would split his time between the two countries until mid-1976. [218]

### In the Aftermath of September 11

Marini now dedicated himself to the MIR's work in the exterior, at a time when military governments, as part of Operation Condor, were working to track down *miristas* in exile.[219] Over time it became clear that he was being monitored by both the Brazilian and Chilean regimes. In fact, the Chilean secret police, DINA, had hatched a plan to capture both Marini and the brother of Miguel Enríquez, Edgardo. The latter would be disappeared a year later in Argentina. Marini nonetheless continued the work he had initiated in Chile, moving throughout Europe and, when possible, Latin America, until the beginning of 1977. He was the main speaker in Frankfurt in a rally commemorating the coup's first anniversary, before a crowd of an estimated 300,000 supporters. From 1974 to 1979, he edited and wrote regularly for the *Correo de la Resistencia,* the MIR's international organ.[220] His work creating "an external rear guard that would help to sustain the political work of the front," who were now targets of the military junta's death squads and

---

217. Kay, "Theotonio dos Santos," 614; Gutiérrez, "Ruy Mauro Marini."

218. Marini, "Memória," 103, 105.

219. Ibid., 103–5.

220. See Marini's editorials and interviews for *Correo de la Resistencia* here: https://marini-escritos.unam.mx/?cat=94.

the DINA, would be central to the MIR's international activity until the end of the dictatorship.[221]

In 1974, Marini took part in founding the journal *Cuadernos Políticos*, with a group of young Mexican intellectuals who had been formed "in the heat of the movement of 1968."[222] According to Marini, Neus Espresate, director of Era publishing house (which had published *Dialéctica*), played an important role as a member of the journal's editorial committee. Marini was likewise a committee member, although because of his earlier experiences in Mexico it would be two years before he felt secure enough to make this public. Later he remarked that the journal's board, whose rich long meetings made it feel more like a working group, was initially on the same page ideologically, but then different tendencies emerged. However, under Espresate's guidance, they found ways to keep working together. "*Cuadernos* knew how to be a stimulating and flexible organ, which opened space to new ideas and new authors, giving oxygen to the intellectual climate of the Mexican left."[223]

In the charged atmosphere following the Chilean coup, one of Marini's main tasks was to respond to the charge that the MIR's turn to armed mass struggle in the midst of the parliamentary process made it ultimately responsible for the coup. Marini refuted this claim in several texts. One of the most popular, "Dos estratégias en el proceso chileno," appeared in the July–September 1974 edition of *Cuadernos Políticos*, and later as a chapter in *El reformismo y la contrarrevolución*.[224] Marini explains there why the MIR remained outside the UP coalition once Allende took office, rather than joining the effort, largely led by the Communist Party of Chile (CPCh), to create a "single leadership of the mass movement" that had brought the UP to power. He begins by explaining the MIR and CPCh's divergent readings of the political

221. Gutiérrez, "Ruy Mauro Marini," 272.

222. Marini, "Memória," 106.

223. Ibid.

224. Ruy Mauro Marini, "Dos estrategias en el proceso chileno," *Cuadernos Políticos* 12 (April–June 1974): 20–39, https://marini-escritos.unam.mx/?p=1257; Marini, *El reformismo*.

conjuncture, which in turn shaped their respective strategic projects and tactics from 1970 onward. Given this divergence, Marini argues, there was no objective basis for a united strategy.

Marini focuses on the class composition of each tendency's revolutionary bloc. The CPCh maintained its line of class collaboration following Allende's election, in an effort to ally the organized sections of the urban and rural working class with middle layers of the bourgeoisie that had been alienated by the new system oriented around big capital. This involved political dialogue with the very party that had been dislodged by Allende, Frei's Christian Democratic Party (DC). The MIR, by contrast, did not believe that the popular movement's demands could or should be reabsorbed in further compromises with capital, particularly given the contradictions that had erupted during the UP's first year of reforms. The shift in Chile's dependent development under the Frei government (i.e., the capitalist penetration of the countryside and piecemeal agrarian reform) had indeed fragmented the bourgeois camp. Nevertheless, the very same process had spurred new forms of mass struggle in the countryside by waged and semi-waged workers excluded from this reform, including Indigenous Mapuche peasants. Along with it came growing militancy of both unionized and non-unionized urban workers, *pobladores* from the peripheral urban communities, and petty bourgeois public sector waged workers.

The CPCh and MIR divided over how to relate to this camp. Whereas the CPCh argued for subordinating the popular effervescence to the UP government in the name of stability, the MIR held that it was not the institutions and traditions of bourgeois democracy that would ensure the stability of Allende's government, but this increasingly revolutionary bloc itself. The MIR's policy of alliances put the organized working class "at its center, [but] include[d] the broad proletarian and semi-proletarian masses of the city and the countryside, as well as the impoverished layers of the petty bourgeoisie." Rather than stabilizing an order anathema to popular interests, what was needed was the "development of a mass power [outside of and as an] alternative to the bourgeois state."[225] When the Chilean bourgeoisie launched its counteroffensive in mid-1972, it was this bloc that became more radical in an effort to meet it. There was an "advance of revolutionary positions within the masses, not only in terms of consciousness, but in their very organization."[226] This included steps toward mass control over production and distribution, self-managed industry in the "cordones industriales," factory and supply-side command structures, popular warehouses, and so on. For the MIR, these expressions of popular power were not only conducive to a revolutionary rupture; they were the only way out of the open class warfare that had brought a military-fascistic government to power. That government represented the interests of the newly recomposed bourgeois bloc, which had the U.S. model of counter-insurgency operating firmly in the background. Marini's essay ends with a call for revolutionary left unity, but also a warning that the strategic errors that led to the original crisis of the UP government were in danger of being repeated.

In a second text, an editorial in *Correo de la Resistencia*, Marini sets out the MIR's position one year into the dictatorship.[227] He challenges the reformist claim that the contradictions unleashed by the military junta in its first year would naturally lead to its demise, as the popular classes came to experience the increasing pressure and violence of its economic reforms. He points out that the Chilean bourgeoisie had a similar strategy during Allende's administration, but did not simply wait passively for the "pear to ripen." Instead, with the active support of U.S. imperialism, the bourgeoisie regrouped and engaged in a strategy of "interfer[ing] permanently in the facts of everyday life," culminating in open class warfare. The MIR thus called for a strategy of actively *making* the regime unviable, through a broad political front of organized mass resistance. Their agenda focused on defending the masses' standard of living, and opposing

---

225. Marini, "Dos estrategias"; see also Gutiérrez, "Ruy Mauro Marini," 270.
226. Marini, "Dos estrategias."
227. Ruy Mauro Marini, "El MIR y las tareas de la revolución chilena," *Correo de la Resistencia, Boletín del MIR en el exterior*, no. 1 (June 1974), https://marini-escritos.unam.mx/?p=2715.

wage squeezes, dismissals, and unpaid overtime, together with a demand for basic democratic freedoms.

Finally, the MIR backed a strategy that would mirror the continental coordination achieved between the military regimes and imperialism, in the form of a Revolutionary Coordinating Junta (Junta de Coordinación Revolucionaria, JCR).[228] The JCR was meant to bring together revolutionary currents from around the Southern Cone, many of whose militants had taken refuge in Allende's Chile. The initiative had some assistance from the international socialist camp, but it relied mostly on the revolutionary Cuban government's moral and material support.[229] The JCR became a primary target of Operation Condor, which aimed to effect its "physical liquidation" through coordinated state terror.[230]

From 1978 to 1979, the MIR's leadership decided to support the Chilean resistance by sending experienced cadres back to the country. Marini was asked to join the MIR's central committee, though not for the first time. He agreed, Gutiérrez suggests in his account of the moment, out of a sense of "historical and ethical responsibility."[231] Marini then returned to the work of political education that he had begun in Chile almost ten years earlier. Now, however, he was doing so in support of the revolutionary struggles that had erupted in Nicaragua, El Salvador, and Peru.[232]

### Class Struggle Under a New State Form

This was also a time of theoretical reflection and transformations in Marini's analysis of the Latin American situation. In the 1974 essay "Dos estrategias en el proceso chileno," Marini had used the concept of "military fascism." However, during the course of the 1970s, he began to distance himself from the term, questioning its relevance

---

228. Ibid.

229. Gutiérrez, "Ruy Mauro Marini," 271–72.

230. Cabieses, "Aniversario"; John Dinges, *The Condor Years: How Pinochet and His Allies Brought Terrorism to Three Continents* (New York: New Press, 2004).

231. Gutiérrez, "Ruy Mauro Marini," 273.

232. Cabieses, "Aniversario."

to the new generation of dictatorship taking shape in the region. In *Memória*, Marini explains how he became

> convinced that the characterization of the Chilean (and Latin American, more generally) counterrevolution as fascism would mystify the real nature of the process and aim to justify the formation of broad fronts, in which the bourgeoisie would tend to take on a hegemonic role. At the time, it appeared to still be possible to struggle for a politics of alliances that did not imply the subordination of the popular forces to the bourgeoisie, since the left still possessed, locally, the capacity to act in Latin America and was on the rise in Western Europe, Africa, and Asia. The defeats that it suffered later led to the triumph of a formulation of the broad front under bourgeois hegemony, which presided over Latin America's redemocratization during the 1980s.[233]

Marini also returned to journalism in the mid-1970s, writing for the Mexico City daily *El Universal,* where his texts were occasionally censored.[234] In 1977, with Cláudio Colombani, he took part in the creation of the Center for Information, Documentation, and Analysis of the Workers' Movement (Centro de Información, Documentación y Análisis del Movimiento Obrero, Cidamo), which he directed from 1977 to 1982. Cidamo was an autonomous institution that brought "young and brilliant" researchers—including many exiles from the region—into a space of collective reflection and theoretical production. Among them were the Chileans Jaime Osorio, Patricia Olave Castillo, and Lila Lorenzo (better known by her political alias, Toña), and Luis Hernández Palacios. Other participants were the Mexicans Francisco Pineda and Maribel Gutiérrez, the Peruvian-Honduran Antonio Murga, the Argentinian Alberto Spagnolo, as well as students and militants from revolutionary movements in Central America.[235]

---

233. Marini, "Memória," 96.
234. Ibid., 110.
235. Ibid., 112–13; Kay, "Theotonio dos Santos," 615.

In this context, Marini initiated another important line of inquiry, building on work he had begun in Chile on historical processes of change and socialist revolution. Now, however, he was motivated by fresh concerns that are hinted at in the passage above: the crisis of socialist strategy and the struggle over the terms of the return to democracy. In such processes of "redemocratization," the left had to contend not only with the bourgeois imperialist counterrevolution, but also more and more, with legitimately democratic movements succumbing to a new style of bourgeois leadership.[236] Marini could observe a growing interest among Latin American intellectuals in European social democracy. Since the early 1970s, the spread of social democratic ideology in the region had benefited from seminars, funding, and collaborative projects with European NGOs. For example, there was a meeting "between the main forces of the Chilean left, excluding the PC and the MIR, [in which] the political nature of social democratic action was perfectly defined."[237]

Some of Marini's texts dealing with the political conjuncture in the late 1970s address the changing nature of the state. He had a special interest in the purposeful substitution of military dictatorships with a specific, *limited* form of democracy, once the utility of the dictatorships to regional patterns of accumulation had run its course.[238] Marini also produced several pieces examining a shift in U.S. policy under the Carter administration. In effect, Carter moved away from the doctrine of counterrevolution and counterinsurgency developed to contain the Cuban Revolution, toward the promotion of a "managed" transition to democracy—a transition to what Samuel Huntington referred to as "governable democracy."[239] Instead of the popular democracy

---

236. Ruy Mauro Marini, "La cuestión del Estado en las luchas de clases en América Latina," *Cuaderno* 44 (1980), Serie Avances de Investigación, CELA, UNAM, https://marini-escritos.unam.mx/?p=2908.
237. Marini, "Memória," 102; Gutiérrez, "Ruy Mauro Marini," 274–75.
238. Marini, "Memória," 111.
239. Marini, "La cuestión." Although less known than U.S. support of the Chilean dictatorship, U.S. support for Brazil's dictatorial regime is no less disquieting. In the early 1970s, during his work with the Trilateral Commission, Harvard

demanded by mass movements, Marini felt that a new "state of four powers" was taking shape in which the bourgeois interests advanced by the dictatorship were still dominant. Now, however, the reconstituted three powers of liberal democracy were joined by a fourth: the armed forces, which threatened to dominate the other three. This novel political formation allowed for new levels of popular mobilization that were unthinkable during the early years of the dictatorship. However, it would also determine the contours of the democratic opening. Marini's thesis, launched at a seminar of left intellectuals, irritated some participants, including Andre Gunder Frank. Marini responded that understanding this novel expression of bourgeois and imperialist power was essential to defining a new radical strategy aimed at defeating the "state of big capital."[240]

### The Pattern of Capital Reproduction in Dependent Formations

In this period, Marini also began to extend the line of research initiated with *Dialéctica de la dependencia*. He did so in the context of both the

---

University's Samuel Huntington (later notorious for his "clash of civilizations" thesis, which helped to shape the dominant ideological justification for the global war on terror) acted as an advisor to the Brazilian dictatorship during Emílio Garrastazu Médici's rule, as well as to the South African Apartheid regime. In this role, he advocated for what he termed "decompression": how to effect a gradual, controlled return to democracy without destabilizing the political (and presumably, capitalist) order in question. Samuel P. Huntington, "Approaches to Political Decompression" [mimeo], 1973. Although Huntington's role should not be overstated, he would later write: "The Brazilian transition to democracy was in many respects a masterpiece of obfuscated incrementalism." He also noted the role of a "younger generation of Brazilian political scientists who—thanks to the Ford Foundation, had been trained during the 1960s at Stanford, UCLA, Harvard, MIT, Michigan and elsewhere—played active roles in developing and articulating ideas that were central to the Brazilian process." Samuel P. Huntington, "One Soul at a Time: Political Science and Political Reform," *American Political Science Review* 82, no. 1 (1988): 3–10. At the time of Marini's work on such transitions, Huntington was serving as Coordinator of Security Planning for the National Security Council in the Carter administration.

240. Marini, "Memória," 111.

UNAM's Center of Sciencies and Humanities (Centro de Ciencias y Humanidades, Facultad de Ciencias Políticas y Sociales), where there was a growing cohort of researchers and students trained by him, and, beginning in 1977, at the National School of Economics (Escuela Nacional de Economía), where he was visiting professor. He also oversaw dissertations of students from throughout the region, including Jaime Osorio's thesis on the Chilean state at the College of Mexico (Colegio de México).[241] Marini's work in this period had three main axes: examining the cycle of capital in the dependent economy;[242] the transformation of surplus value into profit;[243] and the shifting nature of subimperialism in the late 1970s.[244]

The article "El ciclo del capital en la economía dependiente" (which included commentary from Héctor Díaz Polanco and Jaime Osorio) examines the three phases of the cycle of capital, as set out in *Capital*, volume 2, in the dependent economy.[245] These phases are circulation, production, and circulation, as expressed in the formula M-C. . . P . . . C-M. Marini points out the extraordinary role that foreign capital plays in the first circulation phase—sometimes in the form of the money-commodity, as direct or indirect investment, sometimes in the form of concrete means of production—and in the second, production phase, where foreign direct investments obtain extraordinary surplus value through the payment of "wages inferior to the value of labor power." Both extraordinary profits and super-exploitative wages exacerbate the concentration of capital and the distortion of income distribution. That, in turn, distorts the realization of capital in the final

---

241. Marini, "Memória," 107–10.
242. Ruy Mauro Marini, "El ciclo del capital en la economía dependiente," in *Mercado y dependencia*, ed. U. Oswald (Mexico City, Mexico: Nueva Imagen, 1979), https://marini-escritos.unam.mx/?p=1332 .
243. Ruy Mauro Marini, "Plusvalía extraordinaria y acumulación de capital," *Cuadernos Políticos* 20 (April-June 1979): 18–39, https://marini-escritos.unam.mx/?p=1326.
244. Marini, "Memória," 115–18.
245. Marini, "El ciclo"; Karl Marx, *Capital*, vol. 2, trans. David Fernbach (London: Penguin Books, 1992).

phase of circulation, fueling the expansion of luxury good production and the transfer of extraordinary profits abroad, in the form of remittances, interest payments on loans, royalties, etc. These particularities set the cycle of capital in dependent economies apart from the experience of classical industrial economies.

A second essay by Marini from this time period, "Plusvalía extraordinaria y acumulación de capital," examines contemporary controversies surrounding the application of the schema of reproduction in *Capital*, volume 2, to historical and concrete studies of Latin American capitalism.[246] In his *Memoria*, Marini describes how the essay, written as part of a public competition to obtain full professorship at the Escuela Nacional de Economía, deals with the

> specific purpose that [the schemas] fulfill in Marx's theoretical construction—the demonstration of the necessary compatibility of the magnitudes of value produced in the different departments of the economy—and analyze[s] the three premises that have caused so much discussion: a) exclusion from the world market; b) the existence of only two classes; c) the consideration of the degree of labor exploitation as a constant factor.[247]

The essay's final section examines the treatment of these schema in the work of three contemporary economists. Marini would later write that, though probably among the least known of his works, this essay formed "an indispensable complement to the *Dialéctica de le dependencia*, insofar as it expresses the result of investigations that I began in Chile, on the effect of labor super-exploitation in the setting of extraordinary surplus value."[248]

In the heated debate with Cardoso and Serra at this time, Marini

---

246. Marini, "Plusvalía."
247. Marini, "Memória," 117.
248. Marini, "Memória," 117–18. Jaime Osorio, Mathias Luce, Carla Ferreira, Marisa Silva Amaral, and Marcelo Dias Carcanholo all continued to work on the patterns of capital reproduction in dependent economies. See Ferreira, Osorio, and Luce, *Padrão*; Luce, *Teoria*, 85–134.

seemed to take some pleasure in perceiving their "clear worry [that] political amnesty was coming closer and that might open the space for me in Brazil."[249] Political amnesty indeed came for those forced into exile by the dictatorship in 1979. However, it would be another five years before Marini could return home.

### HOME AGAIN: BRAZIL 1984–1997

*Mulher, você vai gostar:*
*Tô levando uns amigos pra conversar.*
*Eles vão com uma fome*
*Que nem me contem;*
*Eles vão com uma sede de anteontem.*
*Salta a cerveja estupidamente*
*Gelada pr'um batalhão*
*E vamos botar água no feijão.*

Honey, you'll like this:
I'm bringing some friends around
    to talk.
They come with a hunger
they won't even tell me about;
They come with a thirst from the day
    before yesterday.
So throw enough beer on, insanely
ice cold, for a battalion,
and let's put water in the beans.

—From "Feijoada Completa," by Chico Buarque. The song is set at a party to welcome back friends from exile—above all, people from mass movements who were driven underground. There are so many coming that it's necessary to water down the beans.

In the final section of his memoir, Marini shares some frank—and at times, seemingly painful—reflections about what he experienced on his return to Brazil. These reflections deal with the alienation of exile and Marini's disquiet regarding the state of Brazilian culture. He observes how the Brazilian bourgeoisie was trying to salvage the model of accumulation developed under the dictatorship, now refitted to neoliberal perspectives and policies; all this despite the turmoil unleashed by the Third World debt crisis that began in Mexico in 1982.

More troubling still were the efforts of Brazilian intellectuals, even on the left, to conform to this new orthodoxy. Marini attributes this to the effects of the dictatorship on the intellectual life of universities: the

---

249. Marini, "Memória," 119.

results of curricula being censored, the stream of propaganda over mass media, and military interventions that not only removed students and academics from campus but "mutilated plans for study, and by means of privatization, even degraded the quality of teaching." The dictatorship also used financial resources (provided through agreements with USAID) to steer students to graduate study in the United States and Europe.[250] While claiming to "broaden the bases of [Brazil's] autonomy in the international sphere," the military's cultural policy had instead led to a loss of identity, as the country swung once again toward liberal thought.[251] Following a visit in the mid-1980s, Marini reported that Brazil,

> despite having had its general movement determined by the same tendencies that ruled Latin America in this period—thus participating in the same process characterized by the swelling of class inequalities, of external dependency, and of state terrorism—did so by accentuating its cultural isolation in relation to the region and launching itself toward a compulsive consumption of ideas fashionable in the United States and Europe.[252]

In this context, Marini uncompromisingly condemned left intellectuals who had been co-opted into silence and conformity, including those who had once opposed the system. In what is perhaps a thinly veiled criticism of Cardoso, he notes:

> The closed environment suffocating the country proved profitable to those who could come and go freely, monopolizing and personalizing ideas that flourished in the intellectual life of the region, adjusting them to the limits set out by the dictatorship. . . . In this context, the majority of the Brazilian left collaborated, in a more or less conscious way, with official policy, closing off the road to the diffusion of issues

250. Ibid., 120.
251. Ibid.; see Garcia and Sá, "Brazil," 385, 389–90.
252. Marini, "Memória," 119.

that had spurred the Latin American left in the 1970s, marked by
political processes of great transcendence and ending in a victorious
popular revolution.[253]

Intellectuals were turning away from the popular forces that had
brought about the epoch of democratization. Marini attributes the
intelligentsia's lack of interest in mass social movements to their desire
to connect with the international forces of social democracy: European
social democratic foundations, U.S.-based research foundations and
funders (whether state or private), and cultural institutions funded by
churches and Christian Democrats. He wrote: "The fight to obtain
resources coming from these [sources] reconstituted the intellectual
elite on totally new bases, without any relation to those—based on
political radicalization and on the rise of mass movements—that had
sustained them in the 1960s."[254]

As mentioned earlier, Marini faced considerable obstacles in his
efforts to return to academic life. Dos Santos observes that, of all his
returning colleagues, it was Marini who was "victim of a systematic
boycott" on return.[255] Bambirra attributes the *de facto* ban on Marini to
Cardoso and Serra's attacks.[256] Nonetheless, after he was blocked from
two Rio de Janeiro institutions for overtly political reasons, Marini was
finally reintegrated into the University of Brasília in 1987. There he
joined the Department of Political Science and International Relations
to teach postgraduate studies. In Brasilia, Marini was reunited with
many of his earliest friends and colleagues, including Bambirra and
dos Santos.[257] He energetically supported efforts to reintegrate other
former professors and instructors who had been forced to leave following the coup, a project Marini saw "as repairing one of the many
arbitrary actions committed by the dictatorship."[258]

---

253. Ibid., 121.

254. Marini, "Memória," 122; see also Ouriques, "Apresentação," 20–21.

255. Theotonio dos Santos, in Kay, "Theotonio dos Santos," 619.

256. Bambirra, "Ruy Mauro Marini," 286.

257. Marini, "Memória," 126–27.

258. Ibid.,127.

Marini's investigations in this period continued work begun earlier in Mexico. That research had examined the effects of the debt crisis and the internationalization of capital on the labor process in various countries during the 1980s.[259] Now, he turned to examining the performance of key manufacturing sectors in Brazil (particularly the auto sector) under the military's policy of incentives and export subsidies.[260] He also returned to the debate around income concentration, which he had identified as a consequence of labor super-exploitation in the 1970s. By the early 1980s, the military's "wage squeeze" policy (an effort to control inflation by manipulating annual wage adjustments, which pushed down real wages and exacerbated income inequality) helped to drive a major upsurge in the workers' struggle and the movement for democratization, especially among industrial workers.[261] Marini's research led him to conclude that the uptick in the workers' struggle in this period succeeded in at least slowing the mechanisms of super-exploitation and income inequality, only then to provoke a shift in accumulation strategies by the Brazilian bourgeoisie toward financial investment, productive restructuring, and neoliberal reform:

> . . . the acceleration of income concentration, which began in the 1960s, lost momentum in the late 1970s and early 1980s, as a result, in my opinion, of the rise of social movements in the country at that time. Everything indicates that the strengthening of the bourgeois bloc in the so-called New Republic [following the return to democracy in 1985], the retraction of productive investments to the benefit of financial speculation and the offensives launched against workers—especially in the economic plans that began in 1986—reversed this tendency [i.e., to slow down income concentration].[262]

Despite the importance of these investigations, Marini felt that his

---

259. Ibid., 113.
260. Ibid., 130.
261. Ricardo Antunes, *O novo sindicalismo no Brasil,* 2nd ed. (Campinas, Brasil: Pontes, 1995), 23–25.
262. Ibid., 129.

research in the late '80s had drifted too far from the objectives and concerns of his main lines of work. In May 1990, coming almost full circle, he returned to Rio de Janeiro on sabbatical to refocus his energies.

The result was Marini's final monograph, *América Latina: Dependência e integração*, which brought together several of his essays on the new contours of dependency under globalization.[263] The first essay in the collection deals with the defeat and dispersion of the popular movements that had fought for democracy, and the destruction of the class-based opposition to the limited bourgeois democracy that followed. A second essay examines the "conversion" of Latin America to neoliberalism following two decades of crisis and the transformation of national economies through productive restructuring, greater specialization, and the new ideology of productive efficiency.[264] Marini characterized such neoliberal policies as "the form and expression of the breakthrough reached in inter-bourgeois struggles by the modern fraction, allied to the international bourgeoisie." A third essay charts the crisis in Latin American economic thought in this same period, which left progressive forces with the options of choosing between neoliberal orthodoxy (that ignored imperialism), CEPAL's national-developmentalism, or the reformist versions of the dependency thesis.

The last essay in the book, which was also published in English in the journal *Social Justice*, charts the history of projects for Latin American unification going back to independence.[265] As against the various proposals for regional economic integration in the early 1990s, *all* aligned with the interests of imperialist centers, Marini backs a form of integration consonant with the popular slogan, "the integration of the peoples":

In this context, Latin America—which faces pressures that tend to tear it apart and open the way for the annexation of its separate pieces—must promote a broader economic space, one capable of

---

263. Ruy Mauro Marini, *América Latina*.
264. Ibid., 56–57.
265. Ruy Mauro Marini, "The Paths of Latin American Integration," *Social Justice* 19, no. 4 (1992): 34–47.

adjusting to the requirements of modern technologies of production. However, this cannot be understood, as it was in the 1960s, as a simple matter of generating relatively dynamic economic sectors that operate as small islands in the ocean of underdevelopment in which the region is submerged. On the contrary, it presupposes the construction of a new economy based on the incorporation of broad sectors of the population as workers and consumers, through a correct targeting of investments, a genuine educational revolution, suppression of the high levels of super-exploitation of labor, and, consequently, a better income distribution.[266]

Marini's efforts to understand the convulsions occurring in the world of work culminated in two important final texts. "O conceito de trabalho produtivo: nota metodológica" was an essay written between 1992 and 1997, in which Marini reviews the development of the concept of "productive labor" and the changing definition of the working class in Marx.[267] This is a highly theoretical work that resonated with some topics in the left's contemporary debates: the rise of organized public sector workers in the 1980s, the weaponization of productivity drives, the flexibilization of contracts and rights, and broad shifts in employment by sector. Marini argues that globalization has entailed a diversification of activities—often displaced from manufacturing to the sphere of circulation and distribution—making it more difficult to define and quantify the working class.[268] He dwells on Marx's claim that workers employed in the circulation phase contribute to capital's profitability by conserving value, comparing this to the role of the range of workers in the services sectors (such as transport and commerce), which exploded under globalization. Marini concludes with a rich passage, highly relevant to a decade in which workers' unity was attacked at every angle:

---

266. Ibid., 45.
267. Ruy Mauro Marini, "O conceito de trabalho produtivo: nota metodológica," in Traspadini and Stedile, *Ruy Mauro Marini—Vida e Obra*, 195–205.
268. Ibid., 202.

To define a social class in a given historical moment, it is not enough .
. . to consider the position that men occupy objectively in the material
reproduction of society. Beyond this, it is necessary to consider social
and ideological factors that determine their consciousness in relation
to the role they believe they play in it. . . . Only in the last instance
does the economic base determine consciousness. And it does so
through concrete social dynamics, that is, through class struggle, in
such a way that, under certain circumstances, even workers who are
not directly included in the working class or who consider themselves alien to it due to their position in economic reproduction, can
identify with its aspirations, incorporating themselves into the labor
movement. . . . This is the reason why all the institutions and mechanisms of the political game that characterize bourgeois society . . .
aim to block this perception; they aim to dissolve the latent unity
among the workers before it takes shape.[269]

In a second text, "Proceso y tendencias de la globalización capitalista," Marini observes how labor super-exploitation has extended
to the advanced centers of accumulation, in a globalized economy in
which the law of value has itself become globalized.[270] International
capital relies on increasing workers' productivity through technological innovation but also, simultaneously, labor super-exploitation. Such
super-exploitation results from the drive for increased productivity
and the intensification of labor. The upshot is that individual capitals
can benefit from extraordinary rates of surplus value and profit.[271] No
longer limited to competition within a given national market, where
extraordinary profits tend to be transitory, the heightened competition between large firms in the globalized market implies a permanent
search for extraordinary profit produced by these means, wherever
they may be. Marini compares this moment to the introduction of new
technologies in European production in the late eighteenth and early

---

269. Ibid., 204–5.
270. Ruy Mauro Marini, "Proceso," 267–68.
271. Ibid., 264.

nineteenth centuries. He suggests that new technologies will unleash a new round in the general law of accumulation, increasing the mass of surplus workers and aggravating their pauperization, while "wringing the labor power" of those still remaining in the formal labor process.[272] However, Marini ends by arguing that the solution remains the same as before: downward pressure on workers can only be challenged through the unification of workers' struggles around the world, "putting in march a radical democratic revolution."[273]

At the end of his memoir, Marini discusses the contemporary reception of his work and of the dependency thesis more generally. On the one hand, he recognizes his younger colleagues' determination to open new theoretical paths in the field of Marxism and dependency theory, despite the crisis posed by the collapse of the Soviet Union. On the other hand, he argues that attacks on MDT are at the heart of the crisis of theory in the neoliberal era:

> The theoretical poverty of Latin America in the 1980s is, to a large extent, the result of the offensive against dependency theory, which prepared the ground for the region's reintegration into the new world system that was beginning to take shape and which is characterized by hegemonic affirmation, at all levels, of the great centers of capitalism.[274]

In 1993, Ruy Mauro took up an invitation to return to Mexico and assume the directorship of CELA. In what was perhaps the most fulfilling project of his later years, Marini oversaw, together with Márgara Millán, the compilation of classical texts of twentieth-century Latin American social and political thought, which would be issued in a four-volume series, *La teoría social latinoamericana*.[275] In his memoir,

---

272. Ibid., 267–68.
273. Ibid., 268.
274. Marini, "Memória," 134.
275. Ruy Mauro Marini and Márgara Millán, eds., *La teória social latinoameri-cana: textos escogidos*, 4 vols. (Mexico, D.F.: Universidad Nacional Autónoma de México, 1994).

Marini describes dependency theory's relation to this large body of thought:

> I must conclude by insisting on a peculiar feature of dependency theory, however it may be judged: its decisive contribution to encouraging the study of Latin America by Latin Americans themselves, and its ability, by reversing for the first time the direction of relations between the region and the great capitalist centers, to make it so that, instead of being on the receiving end, Latin American thought would come to influence the progressive currents of Europe and the United States.[276]

Marini passed away from lymphatic cancer in Rio de Janeiro on July 5, 1997.

---

276. Marini, "Memória," 134.

# REFERENCES

Antunes, Ricardo, *O novo sindicalismo no Brasil* [The New Unionism in Brazil], 2nd ed. Campinas, Brasil: Pontes, 1995.

Bambirra, Vânia, "Ruy Mauro Marini: meu melhor amigo! [Ruy Mauro Marini: My Best Friend!]," in *Ruy Mauro Marini—Vida e Obra*, ed. R. Traspadini and J. P. Stedile. São Paulo: Expressão Popular, 2005.

Bandeira, Luiz Alberto Moniz, *O governo João Goulart: as lutas sociais no Brasil—1961-1964* [The João Goulart Government: Social Struggles in Brazil—1961-1964], 7th ed. Rio de Janeiro: Editora Revan, Editora UnB, 2001.

Cabieses Donoso, Manuel, "Aniversario del Movimiento de Izquierda Revolucionario (MIR): El honor y la rebeldía [Anniversary of the Revolutionary Left Movement (MIR): Honor and Rebellion]," *Rebelión.org*, 2018; https://rebelion.org/el-honor-y-la-rebeldia.

Cardoso, Fernando Henrique, "Notas sobre el estado actual de los estudios sobre dependencia [Notes on the Current State of Studies on Dependence]." Santiago, Chile: Instituto Latinoamericana de Planificación Económica y Social, CEPAL, 1974, https://repositorio.cepal.org/handle/11362/34470.

———."The Consumption of Dependency Theory in the United States," *Latin American Research Review* 12, no. 3 (1977): 7-24.

Cardoso, Fernando Henrique, and Enzo Faletto, *Dependency and Development in Latin America*, trans. Marjory Mattingly Urquidi. Berkeley: University of California Press, 1979.

Ceceña, Ana Esther, "Ruy Mauro Marini: um construtor de caminhos [Ruy Mauro Marini: A Pathfinder]," in *Ruy Mauro Marini—Vida e Obra*, ed. R. Traspadini and J. P. Stedile. São Paulo, Brazil: Expressão Popular, 2005.

Chilcote, Ronald H., *Intellectuals and the Search for National Identity in Twentieth-Century Brazil*. Cambridge, UK: Cambridge University Press, 2018.

Codas, Gustavo, "Mais-valia e modernidade em FHC [Surplus Value and Modernity in Fernando Henrique Cardoso]," *Boletim Quinzena*, no. 240 (1996): 14-17.

Dal Rosso, Sadi, and Raphael Lana Seabra, "A teoria marxista da dependência: papel e lugar das ciências sociais da Universidade de Brasília [The Marxist Theory of Dependency: The Role and Place of the Social Sciences at the University of Brasília]," *Revista Sociedade e Estado* 31 (2017): 1029-50.

Dinges, John, *The Condor Years: How Pinochet and His Allies Brought Terrorism to Three Continents*. New York: New Press, 2004.

Ferreira, Carla, Jaime Osorio, and Mathias Luce, eds., *Padrão de reprodução do capital: contribuições da teoria marxista da dependência* [The Schema of Capital Reproduction: Contributions from the Marxist Dependency Theory]. São Paulo: Boitempo Editorial, 2012.

Frank, Andre Gunder, "The Development of Underdevelopment," *Monthly Review* 18, no. 4 (September 1966): 17–31.

Garcia, Ana, and Miguel Borba de Sá, "Brazil: From the Margins to the Centre?" in *The Essential Guide to Critical Development Studies*, ed. H. Veltmeyer and P. Bowles. London: Routledge, 2018.

Gutiérrez, Nelson Y., "Ruy Mauro Marini: perfil de um intelectual revolucionário [Ruy Mauro Marini: Profile of a Revolutionary Intellectual]," in *Ruy Mauro Marini—Vida e Obra*, ed. R. Traspadini and J. P. Stedile. São Paulo: Expressão Popular, 2005.

Higginbottom, Andy, "Superexplotación y *El Capital*: entre el capitalismo actual globalizado y la plusvalía [Super-exploitation and *Capital*: Between Contemporary Globalized Capitalism and Surplus Value]," in *Marxismos y Resistencias en el Sur Global*, ed. N. Kohan and N. López. Madrid: AKAL, 2022.

———. "Structure and Essence in *Capital I*: Extra surplus-value and the stages of capitalism," *Journal of Australian Political Economy* 70 (summer 2012): 251–70.

Huntington, Samuel P., "Approaches to Political Decompression" (mimeo), 1973.

———. "One Soul at a Time: Political Science and Political Reform," *American Political Science Review* 82, no. 1 (1988): 3–10.

Kay, Cristóbal, "Theotonio Dos Santos (1936–2018): The Revolutionary Intellectual Who Pioneered Dependency Theory," *Development and Change* 51, no. 2 (2020): 599–630.

———. *Latin American Theories of Development and Underdevelopment*. London: Routledge, 1989.

Keen, Benjamin, and Keith Haynes, *A History of Latin America*, 8th ed. London: Wadsworth Cengage, 2009.

Lozoya López, Ivette, *Científicos sociales latinoamericanos en el MIR chileno (1965–1973)* [Latin American Social Scientists in the Chilean MIR (1965–1973)], Santiago, Chile: Ariadna Ediciones, 2020, https://books.openedition.org/ariadnaediciones/7622.

Luce, Mathias Seibel, *Teoria Marxista da Dependência: problemas e categorias—uma visão histórica* [The Marxist Theory of Dependency: Problems and Categories—A Historical Overview]. São Paulo: Expressão Popular, 2018.

Marini, Ruy Mauro, "Brazilian interdependence and imperialist integration," *Monthly Review* 17, no. 7 (1965): 10–23, 26–29.

———. "La dialéctica del desarrollo capitalista en Brasil [The Dialectics of Capitalist Development in Brazil]," *Cuadernos Americanos* 146, no. 3 (1966), https://marini-escritos.unam.mx/?p=1126.

———. "Os movimentos estudantis na América Latina [Student Movements in Latin America]," trans. Jonathan Jaumont, 1970, https://marini-escritos.unam.mx/?p=1272.

———. "La izquierda revolucionario brasileña y las nuevas condiciones de la lucha de clases [The Brazilian Revolutionary Left and the New Conditions of Class Struggle]," in *Diez Años de Insurreción en América Latina,* vol. 2, ed. V. Bambirra. Santiago, Chile: Editorial Prensa Latinoamericana S.A., 1971.

———. "Dialéctica de la dependencia: la economía exportadora [The Dialectics of Dependency: The Export Economy]," *Sociedad & Desarrollo* 1 (enero–marzo 1972): 35–51, http://www.marini-escritos.unam.mx/wp-content/uploads/1991/01/3.3-Diale%CC%81ctica-de-la-dependencia.pdf.

———. "Brazilian subimperialism," *Monthly Review* 23, no. 2. (1972): 14–24.

———. *Dialéctica de la dependencia* [The Dialectics of Dependency]. Mexico, D.F.: Ediciones Era, 1973.

———. "Dialéctica de la dependencia," in *Dialéctica de la dependencia.* Mexico, D.F.: Ediciones Era, 1973.

———. "En torno a *Dialéctica de la dependencia* [On the Dialectics of Dependency]," in *Dialéctica de la dependencia.* Mexico, D.F.: Ediciones Era, 1973.

———. *Subdesarrollo y Revolución* [Underdevelopment and Revolution], 5th ed. Mexico, D.F.: Siglo XXII Editores, 1974.

———. *Il subimperialismo brasiliano* [Brazilian Sub-Imperialism]. Turin, Italy: Einaudi, 1974.

———. "El MIR y las tareas de la revolución chilena [The MIR and the Tasks of the Chilean Revolution]," *Correo de la Resistencia, Boletín del MIR en el exterior,* no. 1 (June 1974), https://marini-escritos.unam.mx/?p=2715.

———. "Dos estrategias en el proceso chileno [Two Strategies in the Chilean Process]," *Cuadernos Políticos* 12 (April–June 1974): 20–39, https://marini-escritos.unam.mx/?p=1257.

———. "El desarrollo industrial dependiente y la crisis del sistema de dominación [Dependent Industrial Development and the Crisis of the System of Domination]," in *El reformismo y la contrarrevolución. Estudios sobre Chile.* Mexico, D.F.: Ediciones Era, 1976, https://marini-escritos.unam.mx/?p=1188.

———. *El reformismo y la contrarrevolución. Estudios sobre Chile* [Reformism and Counterrevolution: Studies on Chile]. Mexico, D.F.: Ediciones Era, 1976.

———. "Las razones del neodesarrollismo (respuesta a F.H. Cardoso & J. Serra) [The Arguments for Neodevelopmentalism (Response to F. H. Cardoso & J. Serra)]," *Revista Mexicana de Sociología* 40 (Número extraordinario, 1978): 57–106.

———. "El ciclo del capital en la economía dependiente [The Cycle of Capital in the Dependent Economy]," in *Mercado y dependencia,* ed. U. Oswald. Mexico, D.F.: Nueva Imagen, 1979, https://marini-escritos.unam.mx/?p=1332.

———."Plusvalía extraordinaria y acumulación de capital [Extraordinary
        Surplus Value and Capital Accumulation]," *Cuadernos Políticos* 20
        (April–June 1979): 18–39, https://marini-escritos.unam.mx/?p
        =1326.
———."La cuestión del Estado en las luchas de clases en América Latina
        [The Question of the State in the Latin American Class Struggle],"
        *Cuaderno* 44 (1980), Serie Avances de Investigación, CELA, UNAM,
        https://marini-escritos.unam.mx/?p=2908.
———.*América Latina: Dependência e integração* [Latin America: Dependency
        and Integration]. São Paulo: Editora Página Aberta, 1992.
———."The Paths of Latin American Integration," *Social Justice* 19, no. 4
        (1992): 34–47.
———."Proceso y tendencias de la globalización capitalista [Process and Trends
        in Capitalist Globalization]," in Ruy Mauro Marini, *América Latina,
        dependencia y globalización: Fundamentos conceptuales Ruy Mauro
        Marini,* 2nd ed., coord. E. Sadir and T. dos Santos, ed. C. E. Martins
        and A. Sotelo V. Bogotá: CLACSO y Siglo del Hombre Editores,
        1997, https://marini-escritos.unam.mx/?p=1531.
———. "Memória: por Ruy Mauro Marini [A Memoir: by Ruy Mauro Marini],"
        in *Ruy Mauro Marini—Vida e Obra,* ed. R. Traspadini and J. P. Stedile.
        São Paulo: Expressão Popular, 2005.
———. "O conceito de trabalho produtivo: nota metodológica [The Concept of
        Productive Labor: A Methodological Note]," in *Ruy Mauro Marini—
        Vida e Obra,* ed. R. Traspadini and J. P. Stedile. São Paulo: Expressão
        Popular, 2005.
———*Subdesenvolvimento e revolução* [Underdevelopment and Revolution],
        trans. F. C. Prado and M. M. Gouvêa. Florianópolis: Insular, 2012.
Marini, Ruy Mauro, and Márgara Millán, eds., *La Teória Social
        Latinoamericana: textos escogidos,*vols. 1–4 [Latin American Social
        Theory: Selected Texts]. Mexico, D.F.: Universidad Nacional
        Autónoma de México, 1994.
Marx, Karl, *Capital: A Critique of Political Economy,* vol. 1., trans. Ben Fowkes.
        London: Penguin, 1990.
———*Capital: A Critique of Political Economy,* vol. 2., trans. David Fernbach.
        London: Penguin, 1992.
———*Capital: A Critique of Political Economy,* vol. 3., trans. David Fernbach.
        London: Penguin, 1991.
Miranda, Orlando, and Pery Falcón, eds., *POLOP: uma trajetória de luta pela
        organização independente da classe operária no Brasil* [POLOP:
        the Trajectory of Struggle for the Independent Organization of the
        Working Class in Brazil], 2nd ed. Salvador, Brazil: Centro de Estudos
        Victor Meyer, 2010.
Olave, Patricia, "Ruy Mauro Marini: mínima cronología [Ruy Mauro Marini:
        A Minimal Chronology]," in P. Olave, ed., *A 40 años de Dialéctica de*

*la dependencia*. Mexico, D.F.: Universidad Nacional Autónoma de México, Instituto de Investigaciones Económicas, 2015.

Ortega, Max, and Ana Alicia Solís de Alba, *La izquierda mexicana, una historia inacaba* [The Mexican Left, an Unfinished Story]. Mexico, D.F.: Editorial Itaca, 2012.

Osorio, Jaime, *Teória marxista de la dependencia: Historia, fundamentos, debates y contribuciones* [Marxist Dependency Theory: History, Foundations, Debates and Contributions]. Mexico, D.F.: Universidad Autónoma Metropolitana (UAM)-Xochimilco, 2016.

———."El marxismo latinoamericano y la teoría de la dependencia [Latin American Marxism and the Theory of Dependency]," in *Teória marxista de la dependencia: Historia, fundamentos, debates y contribuciones*. Mexico, D.F.: Universidad Autónoma Metropolitana (UAM)-Xochimilco, 2016.

Ouriques, Nildo, "Apresentação [Introduction]," in R. M. Marini, *Subdesenvolvimento e revolução*, trans. F. C. Prado and M. M. Gouvêa. Florianópolis, Brazil: Insular, 2012.

Passa Palavra, "Extrema-esquerda e desenvolvimento [The Far Left and Development]," (series), parts 8 and 9, June 3, 2011, https://passapalavra.info/2011/06/95903/.

Prado, Fernando Correa, "Por qué hubo que desconocer a la teoría marxista de la dependencia en Brasil [Why the Marxist Theory of Dependency Had to Be Ignored in Brazil]," in P. Olave, ed., *A 40 años de Dialéctica de la dependencia*. Mexico, D.F.: Universidad Nacional Autónoma de México, Instituto de Investigaciones Económicas, 2015.

Reis F., Daniel Aarão, and Jair Ferreira de Sá, eds., "Organização Revolucionária Marxista-Política Operária [Revolutionary Marxist Organization-Workers' Politics]—ORM-POLOP," in *Imagens da Revolução: documentos políticos das organizações clandestinas de esquerda dos anos 1961 a 1971*. Rio de Janeiro: Editora Marco Zero, 1985.

Seabra, Raphael Lana, "A vocação política da teoria marxista da dependência: uma análise da Política Operária [The Political Vocation of Marxist Dependency Theory: An Analysis of Workers' Politics]," *Latin American Research Review* 55, no. 4 (2020): 662–75.

Serra, José, and Fernando Henrique Cardoso, "Las desventuras de la dialéctica de la dependencia [The Misadventures of the Dialectics of Dependency]," *Revista Mexicana de Sociología* 40 (Número extraordinario, 1978): 9–55.

Weeks, John, and Elizabeth Dore, "International exchange and the causes of backwardness," *Latin American Perspectives* 6, no. 2 (1979): 62–87.

# A Note on the Translation

The publication history of *Dialéctica de la dependencia* is addressed in the previous chapter of this book. The present translation of Marini's landmark essay is the first to be published in English. It is based on the version appearing in the eleventh edition of the 1973 book published by Ediciones Era, under chief editor Neus Esperate, which included both the original essay in its entirety and its postscript. This version was then reproduced in a 2008 anthology of Marini's work compiled by Carlos Eduardo Martins.[1]

The aim of this translation is to strike a balance between remaining faithful to Marini's original wording, and clarity. That is, it tries to remain as close as possible to the original text (particularly so when dealing with Marxist terms and concepts), which was the main priority, while allowing more flexibility when necessary to make Marini's meaning clear to the English-speaking reader. Rare departures from either of these two aims are set off by square brackets or identified as a translator's note [TN] in the footnotes.

---

1. Ruy Mauro Marini, *América Latina, dependencia y globalización: Fundamentos conceptuales Ruy Mauro Marini, Antología y presentación Carlos Eduardo Martins* (Bogotá: Siglos del Hombre, CLACSO, 2008). Available at http://biblioteca.clacso. edu.ar/gsdl/collect/clacso/index/assoc/D10902.dir/Antologia_Marini.pdf.

With the second aim in mind, it is worth noting some choices that were made in close consultation with Jaime Osorio and Mathias Luce. Marini uses derivations of the word *escisión* to discuss the creation of a "divide" or "rift" (the word's closest equivalent in English) between the market nurtured in dependent economies, focused on the consuming of luxury and capital goods, and the consumption needs of the majority population. I used the word "fracture" instead. Similarly, the phrase *fuerza de trabajo* in Marxist texts has various English equivalents. Although usually translated as "labor power," it can also refer to the more sociological "workforce"; here, context determined how it was translated. I have brought the Spanish *articulación* into English as "articulation," meaning a linkage, imbrication, or structural connection. Finally, the adjective *mercantil* was rendered as "commodity" (e.g., commodity production) or "market" (e.g., market laws).

Wherever possible, I located and cited already existing English translations of the secondary sources used by Marini. When these were either not available in English, or when the available English versions were problematic (for example, when a sentence appearing in a French or Spanish edition was missing, or when the English version was inaccurate), I opted to translate the secondary sources that Marini refers to in the original version of *Dialectics* and its postscript. In such cases, my priority was to remain as close as possible to the editions that Marini used himself, rather than, for example, referring to the more accurate versions of Marx's texts appearing in the Marx-Engels *Gesamtausgabe* (MEGA), which Marini did not have access to. I used the Penguin English-language translations of Marx's *Capital* (translated by Ben Fowkes and David Fernbach) and the *Grundrisse* (translated by Martin Nicolaus) for the wording of quotes that Marini himself drew from the Spanish-language edition translated by Wenceslao Roces and published by the Fondo de Cultura Económica. However, passages that Marini drew from the French edition translated and edited by Maximilien Rubel, published by Gallimard, have been translated from the original.

In all cases, I opted to preserve the references to Marini's original sources in the footnotes to allow the reader to follow his line of inquiry.

These appear in square brackets following the English-language sources used in the translation and foreign-language sources that are more readily available than those Marini cited; where there is no such indication, the source used is that cited in Marini's original essay. For the same reason, most chapters of this volume end with their own bibliographies, so that the reader will have a discrete snapshot of the sources that went into creating each text. However, there is a single bibliography for both *The Dialectics of Dependency* and its postscript, *On the Dialectics of Dependency*. This combined bibliography follows the postscript and includes the texts that Marini cited directly in Spanish, French, and English, as well as the materials that had to be consulted and used for the translation.

Jaime Osorio's chapter, "Dialectics, Super-Exploitation, and Dependency: Notes on *The Dialectics of Dependency*," was originally published in Spanish as "Sobre Dialéctica, Superexplotación y Dependencia: Notas acerca de *Dialéctica de la dependencia*," in the journal *Argumentos: Estudios Críticos de la Sociedad* in 2013.[2] It was subsequently published in English in the journal *Social Justice* in 2015, translated by Gregory Shank and Heather Anne Harper.[3] This translation has been updated and edited for inclusion in the current book, and we extend warm thanks to the editors of *Social Justice* for their permission to use the essay.

It was an enormous privilege to be able to flesh out the author's ideas and character, as it emerges in the interstices of his writing, by conversing with people who knew him, and I'm very grateful for the opportunity. I would personally like to thank Jaime Osorio and Mathias Luce for their careful reading and commentaries, exchanges, and patience throughout this process. I'm also very grateful to Felipe Marini for agreeing to the project, and for entertaining what may have seemed like trivial questions regarding his father and family. Warm

---

2. Jaime Osorio, "Sobre Dialéctica, Superexplotación y Dependencia: Notas acerca de *Dialéctica de la dependencia*,"*Argumentos: Estudios Críticos de la Sociedad* 26, no. 72 (2013).

3. Jaime Osorio, "Dialectics, Superexploitation, and Dependency: Notes on *The Dialectics of Dependency*," *Social Justice 42*, no. 1 (2015).

thanks and respect are due to Martin Paddio, Chris Gilbert, Rebecca Manski, and Michael Yates at Monthly Review Press for what has been a wonderfully supportive and receptive publishing process. Likewise, I wish to thank Andy Higginbottom for his endless support and encouragement, and his efforts to deepen my understanding of Marxist theory, Marini's accomplishments, and the spaces in between.

—AMANDA LATIMER

# THE DIALECTICS
# OF DEPENDENCY

---

# ON THE
# DIALECTICS OF
# DEPENDENCY:
# A POSTSCRIPT

# The Dialectics of Dependency[1]

## RUY MAURO MARINI

*[. . .] foreign trade, in so far as it does not just replace elements (and their value), only shifts the contradictions to a broader sphere, and gives them a wider orbit.*

—KARL MARX, *CAPITAL*, VOL. 2[2]

*Accelerating accumulation through a greater development of the productive powers of labor and accelerating it through the greater exploitation of the worker are two completely different processes. . . .*

—KARL MARX, *CAPITAL*, VOL. 1[3]

In their analysis of Latin American dependency, Marxist investigators have generally committed two kinds of deviations: substituting the

1. Source: Ruy Mauro Marini, "Dialéctica de la dependencia," in *Dialéctica de la dependencia* (Mexico, D.F.: Ediciones Era, 1973), 9–77.

2. Karl Marx, *Capital: A Critique of Political Economy*, vol. 2, trans. David Fernbach (London: Penguin, 1992), 544.

3. Karl Marx, *Le capital, Oeuvres, Économie*, vol. 1, trans. Maximilien Rubel (Paris: Nouvelle Revue Française, Gallimard, 1963), ch. 24, section 4, 1104–1105nB.

concrete fact for the abstract concept or adulterating the concept in the name of a reality unwilling to accept its pure formulation. In the first case, the result has been so-called orthodox Marxist studies in which the dynamic of the processes under study is poured into a formal mold incapable of reconstructing it at the level of exposition; and in which the relation between the concrete and the abstract is broken, giving rise to empirical descriptions that run parallel to the theoretical discourse without merging with it. This has occurred, above all, in the field of economic history. The second type of deviation has been more frequent in the field of sociology, where, faced with the difficulty of tailoring reality to categories that have not been specifically designed for it, scholars with a Marxist formation turn simultaneously to other methodological and theoretical approaches; the inevitable consequence of this process is eclecticism, a lack of conceptual and methodological rigor, and an alleged enrichment of Marxism that is rather more like its negation.

These deviations stem from a real difficulty: faced with the parameters of the pure capitalist mode of production, the Latin American economy presents peculiarities that at times appear to be deficiencies, and at others—not always easily distinguishable from the former— deformities. The recurrence of the notion of *precapitalism* in studies of Latin America is therefore not accidental. What should be said is that, even if it really is a matter of capitalist relations that are insufficiently developed, this notion refers to aspects of a reality that will never be able to develop in the same way as did the so-called advanced capitalist economies, due to the former's overall structure and functioning. Rather than precapitalism, therefore, what we have is a *sui generis* capitalism that only makes sense if we examine it from the perspective of the system as a whole, both at the national and, mainly, at the international level.

This is especially true when we refer to modern industrial capitalism in Latin America, as it has taken shape over the past two decades. But in its most general form, the proposition is also valid for the period immediately prior to this, and even for the stage of the export economy. It is obvious that, in the latter case, the inadequacy of the theory weighs heavier than its distortion, but if we want to understand how one formation turns into the other, it is in light of the later form that we must study the earlier one. In other words, it is the knowledge of the particular form that Latin American dependent capitalism ended up taking that illuminates the study of its origins, and allows us to understand the trends that led to this result in an analytical sense.

But here, as always, the truth has a double meaning: if it is true that the study of the most developed social forms sheds light on embryonic ones (or, rephrasing the idea with Marx's words, "Human anatomy contains a key to the anatomy of the ape"),[4] it is also true that highlighting a simple element of the still-insufficient development of a society can help us to understand its more complex form, which includes and subordinates that element. As Marx points out:

> [...] the simplest category can express the dominant relations of a less developed whole, or else those subordinate relations of a more developed whole which already had a historic existence before this whole developed in the direction expressed by a more concrete category. To that extent the path of abstract thought, rising from the simple to the combined, would correspond to the real historical process.[5]

When identifying these elements, Marxist categories must thus be applied to reality as instruments of analysis and anticipations of its further development. On the other hand, these categories cannot replace or mystify the phenomena to which they are applied. For this reason, the analysis must weigh them, without in any way breaking with the thread of Marxist reasoning, grafting foreign bodies onto it which cannot be assimilated by it. Conceptual and methodological rigor: this is what Marxist orthodoxy ultimately comes down to. Any limitation to the process of investigation derived therefrom no longer has anything to do with orthodoxy, but only with dogmatism.

---

4. Karl Marx, *Grundrisse: Foundations of the Critique of Political Economy (Rough Draft)*, trans. Martin Nicolaus (London: Penguin, 1993), 105. [Original: Karl Marx, *Introducción general a la crítica de la economía política, 1857* (Montevideo: Carabella, n.d.), 44.]

5. Karl Marx, *Grundrisse*, 102. [Original: Karl Marx, *Introducción*, 41].

## INTEGRATION INTO THE WORLD MARKET

Forged in the heat of the commercial expansion that nascent capitalism fomented in the sixteenth century, Latin America developed in close consonance with the dynamics of international capital. As a colony producing precious metals and exotic goods, it initially contributed to an increase in commodity flows and to the expansion of the means of payment. That expansion enabled the development of commercial and banking capital in Europe, supported the European manufacturing system, and paved the way for the creation of large-scale industry. The Industrial Revolution, which set all this in motion, coincided with the political independence of Latin America, won during the first decades of the nineteenth century. That development in turn gave rise to a group of countries that, based on the demographic and administrative "nervous system" woven together during the colonial period, came to gravitate around England. The flow of commodities, and later of capitals, had their point of convergence in England: ignoring one another, the new countries would link themselves directly to the English metropole and, in keeping with its requirements, began to produce and export primary goods in exchange for consumer manufactures and—when imports exceeded their exports—debts.[6]

---

6. Until the mid-nineteenth century, Latin American exports remained stagnant, and the Latin American trade balance was in deficit; foreign loans were used to maintain the capacity to import. As exports expanded, and especially when foreign trade began to generate positive balances, the role of foreign debt became that of transferring part of the surplus obtained in Latin America to the metropole. The case of Brazil is revealing: from the 1860s onward, as trade balance accounts became increasingly important, servicing of the foreign debt increased. From 63% of the trade balance in the 1860s, it rose to 99% in the 1880s. Nelson Werneck Sodré, *Formação histórica do Brasil* (São Paulo: Editora Brasiliense, 1968), 262. [Original source: 1964 edition. Note that the figure Marini cites regarding the size of foreign debt payments in the 1860s, using this edition, is 50%.] Between 1902 and 1913, while the value of exports grew by 79.6%, Brazil's foreign debt increased by 144.6%, representing 60% of total public expenditure in 1913. J. A. Barboza-Carneiro, *Situation économique et financière du Brésil: mémorandum présenté à la Conférence Financière Internationale* (Brussels: Société des Nations, 1920).

It is from this moment on that Latin America's relations with European capitalist centers are inserted into a defined structure: the international division of labor, which will determine the course of the region's subsequent development. In other words, it is from then on that dependency takes shape, understood as a relation of subordination between formally independent nations, in the framework of which the relations of production of the subordinate nations are modified or re-created to ensure the expanded reproduction of dependency. Thus, the outcome of dependency cannot be anything other than more dependency, and its liquidation necessarily implies eliminating the relations of production it involves. In this sense, Andre Gunder Frank's well-known formula on the "development of underdevelopment" is impeccable, as are the political conclusions to which it leads.[7] The critiques that have been made of it often represent a step backwards in this formulation, in the name of clarifications that claim to be theoretical, but which do not usually go beyond semantics.

However, and herein lies the real weakness of Frank's work, the colonial situation is not the same as that of dependency. Although there is continuity between the two, they are not homogeneous. As Canguilhem rightly says: "[t]he progressiveness of an advent does not exclude the originality of an event."[8] The difficulty of theoretical analysis lies precisely in capturing this originality and, above all, in discerning the moment in which originality implies a qualitative change. As far as Latin America's international relations are concerned, if, as we have indicated, it played a significant role in the formation of the world capitalist economy (primarily with its production of precious metals in

---

7. See, for example, his essay "Capitalist Underdevelopment or Socialist Revolution [Who Is the Immediate Enemy?]," in *Latin America: Underdevelopment or Revolution?* (New York: Monthly Review Press, 1969), 371–409. [Original: Andre Gunder Frank, "Quién es el enemigo inmediato," *Pensamiento Crítico* 13, 1968.]

8. Georges Canguilhem, *The Normal and the Pathological* (New York: Zone Books, 1991), 87. [Original: Georges Canguilhem, *Lo normal y lo patológico* (Buenos Aires, Siglo XXI, 1971), 60.] On the concepts of homogeneity and continuity, see chapter 3.

the sixteenth and seventeenth centuries, but above all in the eighteenth century, thanks to the coincidence between the discovery of Brazilian gold and the English manufacturing boom),[9] it is only in the course of the nineteenth century, and specifically after 1840, that its articulation with that world economy is fully realized.[10] This can be explained if we consider that it is only with the emergence of large-scale industry that the international division of labor is established on solid grounds.[11]

---

9. See Celso Furtado, *The Economic Growth of Brazil: A Survey from Colonial to Modern Times*, trans. Ricardo W. de Aguiar and Eric Charles Drysdale (Berkeley: University of California Press, 1963), 90–92. [Original: Celso Furtado, *Formación económica del Brasil* (Mexico, DF: Fondo de Cultura Económica, 1962), 90–91.]

10. In a work that greatly minimizes the importance of the world market for capitalism's development, Paul Bairoch observes that only "from 1840–1850 the true expansion of [England's] foreign trade begins; from 1860, exports represent 14% of national income, and this is but the beginning of a national evolution that reaches its peak in the years preceding the war of 1914–1918, when exports become about 40% of national income. The beginning of this expansion marks a shift in the structure of English operations as we saw in the chapter on agriculture: starting in 1840–1850, England will begin to depend more and more on foreign countries for its subsistence." Paul Bairoch, *Revolución industrial y subdesarrollo* (Mexico, D.F.: Siglo XXI, 1967), 285. When it comes to the insertion of Latin America in the world capitalist economy, one must refer to the relation with England, even in cases (such as the Chilean exports of grain to the United States) where the relationship is not direct. The statistics cited above thus help to explain one historian's observation that, "between 1825 and 1850, the level of international trade in Spanish America as a whole rose only slightly." Tulio Halperín Donghi, *The Contemporary History of Latin America*, trans. John Charles Chasteen (London: Macmillan Press, 1993), 86. [Original: Tulio Halperin Donghi, *História contemporánea de América Latina* (Madrid: Alianza Editorial, 1970), 158.]

11. "Modern industry has established the world market, for which the discovery of America paved the way." Karl Marx and Friedrich Engels, *The Communist Manifesto* (London: Penguin, 2002), 221. [Original: Karl Marx and Federico Engels, "Manifiesto del Partido Comunista," en *Obras escogidas,* vol. I (Moscow, Editorial Progreso, 1971), 21.] See also Karl Marx, *Capital: A Critique of Political Economy,* vol. 1, trans. Ben Fowkes (London: Penguin, 1990), 786n. [Original: Karl Marx, *El capital*, vol. I (México, D.F.: Fondo de Cultura Económica, 1946–1947), ch.23, 536n3.] Note that we have tried to draw quotations from this [TN: FCE] edition of *Capital* to make it more accessible for the reader; however, due to

The creation of large-scale modern industry would have been severely hampered had it not relied upon dependent countries, and had instead been built on a strictly national basis. Indeed, industrial development implies a great availability of agricultural goods, which allows part of society to specialize in specifically industrial activity.[12] In the case of European industrialization, recourse to merely domestic agricultural production would have curbed the maximized productive specialization made possible by large-scale industry. The rapid growth of the industrial working class and, in general, of the urban population employed in industry and services, which took place in the industrial countries in the last century, could not have taken place without relying on means of subsistence of farm origin that were provided in large measure by Latin American countries. This was what made possible a deepening of the division of labor and, for industrial countries, specialization as world producers of manufactured goods.

But the role played by Latin America in the development of capitalism was not limited to this: in addition to its capacity to create a worldwide food supply, which appears as a necessary condition of its insertion into the international capitalist economy, it will soon begin contributing to the formation of a market for industrial raw materials, whose importance grows in keeping with industrial development itself.[13] The working class's growth in the central countries and the

---

the shortcomings of either the translation itself or the editions on which it is based, in certain cases we prefer the texts of Marx published under Maximilien Rubel's direction: Karl Marx, *Le capital, Oeuvres* (Paris: Gallimard, 1963). In such cases, we also provide a reference corresponding to the Fondo de Cultura Económica edition. [TN: Similarly, see "A Note on the Translation" in this volume regarding the protocol for translations of *Capital* used in this translation.]

12. "A level of productivity of agricultural labour which goes beyond the individual needs of the worker is the basis of all society, and in particular the basis of capitalist production, which releases an ever growing part of society from the direct production of means of subsistence, transforming them, as Steuart says, into 'free hands' and making them available for exploitation in other spheres." Karl Marx, *Capital,* vol. 3 (London: Penguin, 1991), 921. [Original: Karl Marx, *El capital,* vol. 3, ch. 47, 728.]

13. It is interesting to note that at some point, these same industrial nations begin

even more striking rise in its productivity, resulting from the advent of
large-scale industry, led to a proportionally greater increase in the mass
of raw materials being deployed in the production process.[14] This role,
which would culminate at a later point, is also the one that would prove
the most enduring for Latin America; it is a role that will retain its full
importance even after the international division of labor has reached a
new stage.

What is important to consider here is that the functions fulfilled
by Latin America in the world capitalist economy transcend being a
mere response to the physical requirements driven by accumulation
in the industrial countries. Beyond facilitating the quantitative growth
of these countries, Latin America's participation in the world market

---

exporting their capital to Latin America, applying it to the production of raw
materials and food for export. This is especially evident when the presence of
the United States in Latin America intensifies and begins to displace England.
If we observe the functional composition of the foreign capital present in the
region during the first decades of this century, we see that British capital is concentrated primarily in portfolio investments, especially in public and railway
securities, which typically accounted for three-quarters of the total, whereas the
United States does not allocate more than a third of its investments to operations
of this kind, favoring the application of funds to mining, oil production, and agriculture. See Paul R. Olson and C. Addison Hickman, *Pan-American Economics*
(New York: John Wiley & Sons), ch. 5. [Original: Paul R. Olson and C. Addison
Hickman, *Economía internacional latinoamericana* (México, D.F.: Fondo de
Cultura Económica, 1945), ch. 5.
14. "... an increase in the variable component of the capital employed necessitates
an increase in its constant component too, i.e. both in the available extent of the
conditions of production, such as workshops, implements, etc., and, in particular,
in raw material, the demand for which grows much more quickly than the number
of workers." Karl Marx, *Capital,* vol. 1, 480. [Original: Karl Marx, *El capital,*
vol. 1, ch. 12, 293. TN: Marini notes that in this edition, "variable" (variable),
"constante" (constant), and "materias primas" (raw materials) are italicized.]
Otherwise, whatever the variations that variable capital and the fixed element of
constant capital go through, the expenditure of raw materials is always greater
when the degree of exploitation or the degree of productivity increases. See Karl
Marx, *Capital,* vol. 1, ch. 24, subsection 4. [Original: See Karl Marx, *El capital,*
vol. 1, ch. 22, section 4.]

will contribute to shifting the axis of accumulation in the industrial economy from the production of absolute surplus value to that of relative surplus value; that is, that accumulation will come to depend more on increasing labor's productive capacity than simply the exploitation of the worker. By contrast, the development of Latin American production, which allows the region to contribute to this qualitative shift in the central countries, will be based fundamentally on the increased exploitation of the worker. It is this contradictory character of Latin American dependency, which determines the relations of production of the capitalist system as a whole, that should draw our attention.

## THE SECRET OF UNEQUAL EXCHANGE

The insertion of Latin America into the capitalist economy responds to the demands posed by the shift to the production of relative surplus value in the industrial countries. The latter refers to a form of exploitation of wage labor which, based essentially on the transformation of the technical conditions of production, derives from the real devaluing of labor power. Without delving deeply into this issue, it is worth making some clarifications that relate to our topic.

Essentially, one must dispel the confusion that often arises between the concept of relative surplus value and that of productivity. In fact, despite constituting the condition par excellence of relative surplus value, a greater productive capacity of labor does not itself guarantee an increase in relative surplus value. By increasing productivity, a worker only creates more products in the same amount of time, but not more value; it is precisely this fact that leads the individual capitalist to seek increased productivity, since it allows him to lower the individual value of his commodity in relation to the value attributed to it by the general conditions of production, thus obtaining a surplus value superior to that of his competitors—in other words, an extraordinary surplus value.

That said, this extraordinary surplus value, by being converted into extraordinary profit, alters the general distribution of surplus value among the various capitalists, but it does not modify the degree of exploitation of labor in the economy or in the branch in question; that is, it does not affect the rate of surplus value. If the technological process that permitted the increase in productivity is extended to the remaining firms, and the rate of productivity thus becomes uniform, this does not lead to an increase in the rate of surplus value either: the mass of products will only have increased, without changing their value; in other words, the social value of each unit of the product will fall in proportion to the increase in labor productivity. The effect, then, would be not an increase in surplus value, but rather a decrease.

This is because what determines the rate of surplus value is not the productivity of labor in and of itself, but the degree of exploitation of labor; in other words, the relation between surplus labor time (in which the worker produces surplus value) and necessary labor time (in which the worker reproduces the value of his labor power, that is, the equivalent of his wage).[15] Only by altering this proportion, in a manner favorable to the capitalist (that is, by increasing surplus labor at the expense of necessary labor) can one modify the rate of surplus value. For this to happen, the reduction of the social value of commodities must affect the goods necessary for the reproduction of labor power— that is, wage-goods. Relative surplus value is thus inextricably linked to the devaluation of wage-goods, to which the productivity of labor generally, but not necessarily, contributes.[16]

This digression was necessary to better understand why Latin

---

15. "Labor must . . . possess a certain degree of productivity before it can be extended beyond the time necessary for the producer to secure his subsistence, but it is never this productivity, whatever its degree, that is the cause of surplus value. That cause is always surplus labor, whatever the mode of extorting it may be." Literal translation of the passage in Karl Marx, *Le capital, Oeuvres,* Économie *I* (Paris: Gallimard, 1963), ch. 16, 1008–9; the passage does not appear in the Fondo de Cultura Económica edition, where it would belong in vol. 1, ch. 14, 428. [TN: Nor does it appear in the Penguin edition, where it would belong in *Capital,* vol. 1, ch. 16, 647.]

16. See Karl Marx, *Capital,* vol. 1, sections 4, 5, and appendix ("Result of the Immediate Process of Production"). [Original: See Karl Marx, *El capital,* vol. 1, section 4 and 5; Karl Marx, *El capital, Libro I, Capítulo VI* (unpublished) (Buenos Aires: Signos, 1971), part 1.]

America's insertion into the world market contributed to developing the specifically capitalist mode of production, based on relative surplus value. We have already mentioned that one task assigned to Latin America, within the framework of the international division of labor, was providing the industrial countries with the food required for the growth of the working class, in particular, and of the urban population, more generally, that was taking place there. The world's food supply, which Latin America helped to create and which reached its peak in the second half of the nineteenth century, would be a crucial element leading industrial countries to entrust their needs for the means of subsistence to foreign trade.[17] The effect of this supply (magnified by a fall in the prices of primary products on the world market, to which we shall return later) would be to reduce the real value of labor power in the industrial countries, which allowed increases in productivity there to be translated into increasingly higher rates of surplus value. In other words, through its incorporation into the world market for wage-goods, Latin America played a significant role in increasing relative surplus value in industrial countries.

Before examining the other side of the coin, that is, the internal conditions of production that allowed Latin America to fulfill this role, it should be pointed out that it is not only in the sphere of its own economy that Latin American dependency proved to be contradictory: Latin America's participation in the progress of the capitalist mode of production in the industrial countries will, in turn, be contradictory. As indicated earlier, this is because an increase in the productive capacity of labor implies a more than proportional increase in the consumption of raw materials. To the extent that this greater productivity is effectively accompanied by greater relative surplus value, this means that the value of variable capital falls in relation to that of constant capital (which includes raw materials); in other words, that the value-composition of capital rises. Now, what the capitalist appropriates directly is

---

17. By 1880, the share of imports [TN: "exports" in the original] in England's food consumption was 45% for wheat, 53% for butter and cheese, 94% for potatoes, and 70% for meat. Data from M. G. Mulhall, in Bairoch, *Revolución industrial y subdesarrollo*, 248–49.

not the surplus value produced, but rather the part that corresponds to him in the form of profit. Since the rate of profit cannot be determined in relation to variable capital alone, but rather in relation to the total capital advanced in the process of production (that is, wages, facilities, machinery, raw materials, etc.), the result of the increase in surplus value tends to be—provided it implies, even in relative terms, a simultaneous rise in the value of the constant capital employed to produce it—a fall in the rate of profit.

This contradiction, which is crucial for capitalist accumulation, is countered by means of various procedures which, from the strictly productive point of view, are oriented either toward increasing surplus value even more, in order to compensate for the decline in the rate of profit; or toward inducing a parallel decline in the value of constant capital, with the aim of preventing the decline from taking place. Among the second kind of procedures, our interest here is in the role of the worldwide supply of industrial raw materials, which appears as a counterpart—from the perspective of the value composition of capital—to the world supply of foodstuffs. As in the latter case, it is by increasing an ever-cheaper mass of products on the international market that Latin America not only fuels the quantitative expansion of capitalist production in the industrial countries, but also contributes to overcoming the pitfalls that the contradictory nature of capital accumulation creates for that expansion.[18]

---

18. Marx summarizes this as follows: "In so far as foreign trade cheapens on the one hand the elements of constant capital and on the other the necessary means of subsistence into which variable capital is converted, it acts to raise the rate of profit by raising the rate of surplus-value and reducing the value of constant capital." Marx, *Capital,* vol. 3, 344. [Original: Karl Marx, *El capital,* vol. 3, ch. 14, 236]. It should be borne in mind that Marx does not limit himself to this observation, but also illustrates the contradictory way that foreign trade contributes to lowering the rate of profit. We will not follow him, however, down this path, nor pursue his concern over how profits obtained by capitalists operating in the sphere of foreign trade may raise the rate of profit (a procedure that could be classified as a third kind of measure counteracting the tendency for the rate of profit to fall, alongside the growth of shareholder capital: measures aimed at circumventing the rate of profit's tendential decline by displacing capital to non-productive spheres). Our

There is, however, another aspect of the problem that must be considered. This is the well-known fact that the increase in the world supply of food and raw materials has been accompanied by a decline in the prices of these products, relative to the prices of manufactured goods.[19] Since the price of industrial products remains relatively stable, and in any case declines slowly, the deterioration in the terms of trade in fact reflects the depreciation of primary goods. It is clear that such a depreciation cannot correspond to the real devaluation of these goods, due to increased productivity in the non-industrial countries, since it is precisely there that productivity rises most slowly. It is thus worth investigating the reasons for this phenomenon, as well as the reasons why it did not become a disincentive to Latin America's incorporation into the international economy.

The first step in answering this question is to discard simplistic explanations that refuse to see anything other than the results of the law of supply and demand. Although competition clearly plays a decisive role in determining prices, it does not explain why, on the side of supply, it expands in an accelerated way regardless of whether the terms of trade are deteriorating. Nor can the phenomenon be properly explained if we limit ourselves to the empirical observation that market laws have been distorted at the international level due to diplomatic and military pressure on the part of the industrial nations. This reasoning, although based on real facts, inverts the order of explanation, and fails to recognize that behind the use of extra-economic pressure

---

purpose here is not to delve into an examination of the contradictions of capitalist production in general, but only to clarify the fundamental causes of Latin American dependency.

19. Referring to statistics from the United Nations Economic Department, Paolo Santi notes, with respect to the relation between the prices of raw materials and manufactures: "Setting the five-year period 1876–1880 = 100, the index drops to 96.3 in the period 1886–1890, to 87.1 in the years 1896–1900, and stabilizes in the period from 1906 to 1913 at 85.8, starting to fall, and all the more quickly, following the end of the war." Paulo Santi, "El debate sobre el imperialismo en los clásicos del marxismo," in *Teoría marxista del imperialismo* (Córdoba: Cuadernos de Pasado y Presente, 1969), 49.

is an economic base that makes it possible. Both kinds of explanation, therefore, help to conceal the nature of the phenomena under study, and give rise to illusions about the real nature of international capitalist exploitation.

It is not because the non-industrial nations were abused that they have become economically weak; it is because they were weak that they were abused. Nor is it because they produced more than they should have that their trading position deteriorated; rather, it was the deterioration in trade that forced them to produce on a larger scale. To refuse to see things in this way is to mystify the international capitalist economy; it is to make people believe that that economy could be different from what it really is. Ultimately, this leads to a call for equitable trade relations between nations, when what is at issue is the need to abolish international economic relations based on exchange value.

Indeed, as the world market attains a more developed form, the use of political and military violence to exploit weak nations becomes superfluous, and international exploitation can rely increasingly on the reproduction of economic relations that perpetuate and amplify the backwardness and weakness of those nations. We see the same phenomenon here that is observed internally in the industrial economies: the use of force to subject the working masses to the rule of capital diminishes as economic mechanisms that enshrine that subordination come into play.[20] The expansion of the world market provides the basis

---

20. "It is not enough that the conditions of labour are concentrated at one pole of society in the shape of capital, while at the other pole are grouped masses of men who have nothing to sell but their labour-power. Nor is it enough that they are compelled to sell themselves voluntarily. The advance of capitalist production develops a working class which by education, tradition and habit looks upon the requirements of that mode of production as self-evident natural laws. The organization of the capitalist process of production, once it is fully developed, breaks down all resistance. The constant generation of a relative surplus population keeps the law of the supply and demand of labour, and therefore wages, within narrow limits which correspond to capital's valorization requirements. The silent compulsion of economic relations sets the seal on the domination of the capitalist over the worker. Direct extra-economic force is still of course used, but only in exceptional cases. In the ordinary run of things, the worker can be left to the

for the operation of the international division of labor between industrial and non-industrial nations, but the counterpart of that division is
the expansion of the world market. The development of commodity
relations lays the foundation for a fuller application of the law of value
to take place, but it simultaneously creates all the conditions for the
various mechanisms through which capital tries to evade this law.

In theory, commodity exchange implies the exchange of equivalents,
the value of which is determined by the amount of socially necessary
labor embodied in the commodities. In practice, one can observe various mechanisms that allow value transfers to take place, bypassing the
laws of exchange mechanisms expressed in the way market prices and
the prices of production of commodities are set. A distinction must be
made between mechanisms operating within the same sphere of production (whether of manufactured goods or raw materials) and those
operating in distinct but interrelated spheres. In the first case, the
transfers correspond to specific applications of the laws of exchange;
in the second, they more openly adopt the character of transgressing
such laws.

Thus, as a result of greater labor productivity, a nation can have
prices of production that are lower than those of its competitors, without significantly lowering the market prices that those competitors'
conditions of production have helped to establish. For the favored
nation, this is expressed as an extraordinary profit, similar to what we
observed when examining how individual capitals appropriate the
fruits of labor productivity. It is only natural that the phenomenon
appears above all at the level of competition among industrial nations
and less so among those producing primary goods, since capitalist laws
of exchange operate most fully among the former. This is not to say that
it does not occur among the latter, especially once capitalist relations of
production have developed there.

In the second case—transactions between nations exchanging

'natural laws of production,' i.e. it is possible to rely on his dependence on capital,
which springs from the conditions of production themselves, and is guaranteed in
perpetuity by them." Karl Marx, *Capital*, vol. 1 (London: Penguin, 1990), 899.
[Original: Karl Marx, *El capital*, vol. 1, ch. 24, 627.]

different kinds of commodities, such as manufactures and raw materials—the mere fact that some produce goods that the rest do not, or cannot produce as easily, allows the former to evade the law of value; that is, to sell their products at prices higher than their value, thus giving rise to an unequal exchange. This implies that the disadvantaged nations must freely cede part of the value they produce, and that this concession or transfer is made even greater in favor of the country that sells commodities to them at the lowest price of production, by virtue of its greater productivity. In the latter case, the transfer of value is twofold, although it does not necessarily appear so to the nation transferring value, inasmuch as its different suppliers can all sell at the same price, regardless of the fact that the profits realized are distributed unequally among them and that most of the value ceded is concentrated in the hands of the country with the highest productivity.

Faced with these mechanisms of value transfer, whether based on productivity or a monopoly of production, one can identify—always in the sphere of international market relations—a compensatory mechanism. This is the recourse to an increase in the value exchanged, on the part of the disadvantaged nation: without preventing the transfer of value based on the mechanisms described above, this makes it possible to totally or partially neutralize it by increasing the value realized. Such a compensatory mechanism can be observed both in the exchange of similar products and in the exchange of products originating in different spheres of production. We are concerned here only with the second case.

What matters is that, to increase the mass of value produced, the capitalist must inevitably resort to a greater exploitation of labor, either by increasing its intensity, or by prolonging the working day, or finally, by combining the two procedures. Strictly speaking, only the first method—an increase in the intensity of labor—really counteracts the disadvantages that result from lower labor productivity, since it allows for the creation of more value in the same amount of working time. In fact, all these methods help to increase the mass of value realized, and accordingly, the amount of money obtained through exchange. This is what explains, at this level of analysis, why the world supply of raw materials and foodstuffs increases as the margin between their market prices and the real value of production widens.[21]

What becomes clear, then, is that nations disadvantaged by unequal exchange do not so much seek to correct the imbalance between the prices and value of their exported commodities (which would imply a redoubled effort to increase labor's productive capacity), but rather to compensate for the loss of income created by international trade, by resorting to a greater exploitation of the worker. We thus reach a point where it is no longer sufficient for us to continue to deal simply with the notion of exchange between nations. Rather, we must face the fact that, within the framework of this exchange, the appropriation of the value realized masks the appropriation of a surplus value which is generated through the exploitation of labor within each nation. From this angle, the transfer of value is a transfer of surplus value that appears, from the point of view of the capitalist operating in the disadvantaged nation, as a decrease in the rate of surplus value, and thus in the rate of profit. Hence, the counterpart of the process by which Latin America helped to increase the rate of surplus value and the rate of profit in the industrial countries implied precisely the opposite effects for the region itself. And what appeared to be a compensatory mechanism in the market sphere is in fact a mechanism operating in the sphere of domestic production. Hence, we must shift the focus of our analysis to that sphere.

---

21. Celso Furtado has ascertained this phenomenon, without deriving all the implications that follow from it: "The decline in Brazilian export prices between 1821–1830 and 1841–1850, was about 40 per cent. For imports, the price index for British exports may be considered as a fairly good source. This index remained perfectly stable between the two decades. Thus the decline in the index of terms of trade amounted to approximately 40 per cent—in other words, real income from exports grew 40 per cent less than their physical volume. As the average annual value of exports increased from £3,900,000 to £5,470,000—a 40 percent growth—real income derived from the exporting sector grew in the same proportion, whereas the production effort in this sector approximately doubled." Furtado, *The Economic Growth of Brazil*, 117. [Celso Furtado, *Formación económica del Brasil*, 115.]

## THE SUPER-EXPLOITATION OF LABOR

We have seen that the problem that unequal exchange poses for Latin America is not precisely that of counteracting the transfer of value it implies, but rather that of compensating for a loss of surplus value; and that, unable to prevent this loss at the level of market relations, the dependent economy reacts by compensating for it at the level of domestic production. The increase in the intensity of labor appears, from this perspective, as an increase in surplus value achieved through greater exploitation of the worker and not through an increase in his productive capacity. The same could be said of prolonging the working day; that is, the increase in absolute surplus value in its classic form. Unlike the former, this is a matter of simply increasing surplus labor time, the time in which the worker continues to produce after having created a value equivalent to that of the means of subsistence for his own consumption. Finally, there is a third procedure, which consists of reducing the worker's consumption beyond its normal limit, so that "it transforms the worker's necessary fund for consumption, within certain limits, into a fund for the accumulation of capital,"[22] which implies a specific mode of increasing surplus labor time.

Here, we should clarify that our use of categories referring to the appropriation of surplus labor under capitalist relations of production is not meant to imply that the Latin American export economy was already operating based on capitalist production. We employ these categories in the spirit of the methodological observations laid out at the beginning of this study; that is, because they allow us to better characterize the phenomena under study, and also because they suggest the direction in which they lead. Moreover, it is not strictly necessary for unequal exchange to exist for the above-mentioned mechanisms of extracting surplus value to come into play; the simple fact of being linked to the world market, and the ensuing conversion of the production of use values into that of exchange values that this entails, immediately unleashes a desire for profit that becomes all the more unbridled the more backward the existing mode of production. As Marx notes,

---

22. Karl Marx, *Capital*, vol. 1, 748. [Karl Marx, *El capital*, vol. 1, ch. 24, 505.]

[...] as soon as peoples whose production still moves within the lower forms of slave-labor, the *corvée*, etc. are drawn into a world market dominated by the capitalist mode of production, whereby the sale of their products for export develops into their principal interest, the civilized horrors of over-work are grafted onto the barbaric horrors of slavery, serfdom, etc.[23]

The effect of unequal exchange is to exacerbate the desire for profit—to the extent that it places obstacles in the way of its full satisfaction—and thus to intensify the methods of extracting surplus labor.

Having said that, the three mechanisms identified—the intensification of work, the extension of the working day, and the expropriation of part of the labor necessary for the worker to replenish his labor power—give rise to a mode of production based exclusively on the greater exploitation of the worker, and not on the development of his productive capacity. This is consistent with the low level of development of the productive forces in the Latin American economy, but also with the kinds of activities that are carried out there. Indeed, more than in manufacturing industry, where increased labor implies at least a greater use of raw materials, in extractive industries and in agriculture, the effect of increased labor on the elements of constant capital is much smaller, since it is possible, through the mere action of man upon nature, to increase the wealth produced without additional capital.[24] It is understood that in these circumstances, productive activity is based

---

23. Marx adds, "Hence the Negro labour in the southern states of the American Union preserved a moderately patriarchal character as long as production was chiefly directed to the satisfaction of immediate local requirements. But in proportion as the export of cotton became of vital interest to those states, the over-working of the Negro, and sometimes the consumption of his life in seven years of labour, became a factor in a calculated and calculating system. It was no longer a question of obtaining from him a certain quantity of useful products, but rather the production of surplus-value itself. The same is true of the *corvée*, in the Danubian Principalities for instance." Karl Marx, *Capital*, vol. 1, ch. 10, section 2, 345. [Original: Karl Marx, *El capital*, vol. 1, ch. 8, 181.]

24. See Karl Marx, *Capital*, vol. 1, ch. 24, section 4, 751–52. [Original: See Karl Marx, *El capital*, vol. 1, ch. 22, section 4, 508–9.]

primarily on the extensive and intensive use of labor power: this makes it possible to lower the value composition of capital, which, combined with intensifying the degree of labor exploitation, causes the rates of surplus value and of profit to rise simultaneously.

It is also important to note that, in the three mechanisms considered, the essential feature is that the worker is denied the conditions necessary to replenish his labor power that has been worn away: in the first two cases, this is because the worker is forced to expend more labor power than he would normally provide, leading to his premature exhaustion; in the last case, it is because even the possibility of consuming what is strictly necessary to maintain his labor power in a normal state is taken away. In capitalist terms, these mechanisms (which, moreover, can and usually do occur in combination) mean that labor [power] is remunerated below its value,[25] and thus amount to a super-exploitation of labor.

This explains why it was precisely in those areas dedicated to export production where the wage labor regime was first imposed, initiating the process of transforming the relations of production in Latin America. It is useful to bear in mind that capitalist production presupposes the direct appropriation of labor power, and not only of the products of labor; in this sense, slavery is a mode of labor more suited to capital than servitude, and it is therefore not accidental that the colonial enterprises directly connected with European capitalist centers—such as the gold and silver mines of Mexico and Peru, or the sugarcane plantations of Brazil—were based on slave labor.[26] However,

---

25. "Any variation in the magnitude of labour, whether extensive or intensive . . . affects the value of labour power, to the extent that it hastens its wear and tear." Karl Marx, *Le capital, Oeuvres,* Économie *1,* ch. 17, section 2, 1017. See also Karl Marx, *Capital,* vol. 1, 661. [Original: Karl Marx, *Le capital, Oeuvres,* vol. 1, ch. 17, section 2, 1017; Karl Marx, *El capital,* vol. 1, ch. 15, section 2, 439.]

26. A similar phenomenon appears in Europe at the dawn of capitalist production. Just by taking a closer look at how the passage from feudalism to capitalism took place there one realizes that the worker's condition, on leaving the state of servitude, resembles more that of the enslaved person than that of the modern wage worker. See Karl Marx, *Capital*, vol. 1, ch. 26. [TN: See, for example, pp.

apart from scenarios in which the labor supply is totally elastic (which was not true of slave labor in Latin America, from the second half of the nineteenth century onward), the regime of slave labor constitutes an obstacle to the indiscriminate lowering of the worker's remuneration.

> In the case of the slave, the *minimal wage* appears as a constant quantity, independent of his work. In the case of the free laborer, the *value of his labor power* and the *average wage* corresponding to it are not contained within those predestined limits, independent of his own labor, determined by his purely physical needs. The *average* remains more or less *constant* for the *class as a whole*, like the value of all commodities; but it does not immediately appear so to the *individual* worker, whose wages may be above or below this minimum.[27]

In other words, the regime of slave labor, leaving aside exceptional labor market conditions, is incompatible with the super-exploitation of labor. The same is not true of wage labor and, to a lesser degree, servile labor.

Let us insist on this point. The superiority of capitalism over other forms of commodity production, and its basic difference from them, lies in the fact that what it transforms into a commodity is not the worker—that is to say, the total time of the worker's existence, with all the dead time that this implies from the point of view of production—but rather the worker's labor power, meaning the time of his existence that is usable for production, leaving to the worker himself the responsibility for time that is non-productive from the capitalist point of view. This explains why, when a slave-based economy is subordinated to the world capitalist market, the exploitation of the slave is intensified, since the owner now has an interest in reducing any downtime in

---

875-76.] [Original: Karl Marx, *El capital*, vol. 1, ch. 28.]

27. Karl Marx, *El capital, Libro 1, Capítulo 6 (inédito)* (Buenos Aires, Signos, 1971), 68-69, italics in the original. [TN: This is a direct translation of the quotation in Marini's essay taken from the Editora Signos edition of *El capital*, which we found preferable to the Penguin edition's problematic translation of the passage that begins, "In the eyes of the slave. . . . "]

production, and making productive time coincide with the time of the worker's own existence.

But, as Marx notes, "[t]he slave-owner buys his worker in the same way he buys his horse. If he loses his slave, he loses a piece of capital, which he must replace by fresh expenditure on the slave-market."[28] The super-exploitation of a slave, which prolongs his workday beyond tolerable physiological limits and necessarily results in his premature exhaustion through death or incapacity, can only occur, therefore, if it is possible to easily replace the worn-out laborer.

> The rice-grounds of Georgia, or the swamps of the Mississippi, may be fatally injurious to the human constitution; but the waste of human life which the cultivation of these districts necessitates, is not so great that it cannot be repaired from the teeming preserves of Virginia and Kentucky. Considerations of economy, moreover, which, under a natural system, afford some security for humane treatment by identifying the master's interest with the slave's preservation, when once trading in slaves is practised, become reasons for racking to the uttermost the toil of the slave; for, when his place can at once be supplied from foreign preserves, the duration of his life becomes a matter of less moment than its productiveness while it lasts.[29]

Evidence to the contrary proves the same thing: when the coffee boom was beginning in Brazil in the second half of the last century, the fact that the slave trade had been suppressed in 1850 made slave labor so unattractive to southern landowners that they preferred to resort to the regime of wage-labor, through European immigration, and also favored policies aimed at suppressing slavery. We should recall that a significant part of the slave population was located in the decadent sugar-producing zone of the northeast, and that the development of agrarian capitalism in the south required their liberation, in order to

---

28. Karl Marx, *Capital*, vol. 1, ch. 10, 377. [Original: Karl Marx, *El capital*, vol. 1, ch. 8, section 5, 208.]

29. John Elliot Cairnes, quoted in Karl Marx, *Capital*, vol. 1, ibid. [Original: Cairnes quoted in Karl Marx, *El capital*, vol. 1, 209, italics in original.]

constitute a free labor market. The creation of this market, with the law abolishing slavery in 1888, which followed a series of gradual measures in that direction (such as the status of free men granted to the children of slaves, among others), is a most interesting phenomenon. On the one hand, it was taken to be an extremely radical measure, liquidating the foundations of imperial society (the monarchy would survive for little more than a year after the passing of the 1888 law) and even went so far as to deny former slave owners any kind of compensation. On the other, it sought to offset its impact with measures aimed at tying the worker to the land (the inclusion of an article in the Civil Code binding people to the debts they had incurred; the *barracão* [truck] system, allowing the *latifundista* a true monopoly over the trade in consumer goods inside the hacienda, etc.), and the granting of generous credits to affected landowners.

The mixed system of servitude and wage labor established in Brazil, as the export economy developed for the world market, is one of the ways by which Latin America arrives at capitalism. One can see how the form taken by the relations of production there is not so different from the labor regime established, for example, in Chilean saltpeter mines, whose token system [*sistema de fichas*] corresponds to the [Brazilian] *barracão*. In other contexts, particularly in the process of subordinating a country's interior to its export zones, the relations of exploitation are more evidently servile relations. Here, the sacking of the surplus product for the sake of commercial or usurious capitalist accumulation sees the worker involved in direct exploitation by capital, which tends to assume the character of super-exploitation.[30] For the capitalist, however, servitude has the disadvantage of not allowing him

---

30. It is for this reason that Marx refers to countries "where labour is not yet formally subsumed by capital although in reality the worker is already exploited by the capitalist," exemplifying this with the case of India, "where the ryot operates as an independent peasant farmer, and his production is not yet subsumed under capital, although the money-lender may well extort from him in the form of interest not only his entire surplus labour, but even—to put it in capitalist terms—a part of his wages." Karl Marx, *Capital*, vol. 3, 321. [Original: Karl Marx, *El capital*, vol. 3, ch. 13, 216.]

to directly manage production, and always raises the possibility, even if only theoretical, that the immediate producer will emancipate himself from the relation of dependence in which the capitalist has placed him.

It is not, however, our purpose here to study the particular economic forms that existed in Latin America before it effectively entered the capitalist stage of production, nor the ways that this transition took place. We intend only to establish the guidelines with which this study is to be carried out, which correspond to the actual movement of the formation of dependent capitalism: *from circulation to production; from the connection to the world market to the impact that this had on the internal organization of work; and then to return to reconsider the problem of circulation*. For it is characteristic of capital to create its own mode of circulation, and the expanded, worldwide reproduction of the capitalist mode of production depends on this:

> [...] since capital alone possesses the conditions of the production of capital, since it alone satisfies these conditions and strives to realize them, its general tendency is to form everywhere the grounds of circulation, the productive centers of the same, and to assimilate them into itself; in short, to transform them into centers of production that are virtually or effectively creators of capital.[31]

Once converted into a capital-producing center, Latin America will thus have to create *its own mode of circulation,* which cannot be the same as that engendered by industrial capitalism and which gave rise to its dependency. To constitute a complex whole, it is necessary to resort to simple elements that can be combined with each other, but which are not identical. The task of understanding the specificity of the cycle of capital in the Latin American dependent economy thus entails illuminating the very foundation of its dependence in relation to the world capitalist economy.

---

31. TN: Here, the passage is translated from the Rubel translation that Marini used simply because it is clearer than the passage from the Penguin edition (found on page 542). See Karl Marx, "Principes d'une critique de l'économie politique," *Oeuvres,* Économie 2 (Paris: Gallimard, 1968), 254.

## THE CYCLE OF CAPITAL IN THE
## DEPENDENT ECONOMY

By developing its commodity production in response to the world market, Latin America is led to internally reproduce relations of production that existed at the origin of this market, which determined its character and expansion.[32] But this process was marked by a profound contradiction: called upon to contribute to capital accumulation based on the productive capacity of labor in the central countries, Latin America would have to do so through accumulation based on the super-exploitation of its workers. In this contradiction resides the essence of Latin American dependency.

The real basis for this development are the ties linking the Latin American economy to the world capitalist economy. Born to meet the demands of capitalist circulation—whose axis of articulation is constituted by the industrial countries—and focused on the world market, Latin American production does not depend on internal consumption capacity for its realization. Thus, from the dependent country's point of view, a separation takes place between the two fundamental moments in the cycle of capital—the production and circulation of commodities. The effect of this is to make it so that the contradiction inherent to capitalist production in general appears in a specific way in the Latin American economy; that is, the contradiction that sets capital in opposition to the worker as a seller and buyer of commodities.[33]

---

32. We have already pointed out how this initially occurs at the most immediate points of connection with the world market; the capitalist mode of production only progressively (and even today, in an unequal way) subordinates the economy as a whole.

33. "Contradiction in the capitalist mode of production. The workers are important for the market as buyers of commodities. But as sellers of their commodity—labour-power—capitalist society has the tendency to restrict them to their minimum price." Karl Marx, *Capital,* vol. 2, 391n1. [Original: Karl Marx, *El capital,* vol. 2, ch. 16, section 3, 283n1.] In this note, Marx reveals his intention to address the theory of workers' underconsumption in the following section, but, as Maximilien Rubel observes, he does not see this through. Karl Marx, *Le capital, Oeuvres,* Économie 2, 1715. Some elements had been set out in the *Grundrisse.*

This is key to understanding the character of the Latin American economy. Initially, one should consider that, in the industrial countries, whose capital accumulation is based on the productivity of labor, there is a real opposition generated by the dual character of the worker—as producer and consumer—but that opposition is to a certain extent counteracted by the form that the cycle of capital takes. Thus, although capital privileges the worker's productive consumption (that is, the consumption of the means of production implied in the labor process) and tends to disregard his individual consumption (that the worker uses to replenish his labor power), which capital sees as unproductive consumption,[34] this occurs exclusively at the moment of production. When the realization phase begins, this apparent contradiction between the workers' individual consumption and the reproduction of capital disappears, as soon as this consumption (added to that of capitalists and of unproductive strata in general) restores to capital the form it needs to begin a new cycle, that is, the money form. The individual consumption of the workers thus represents a decisive element in the creation of demand for the commodities produced, and is one of the conditions for the flow of production to be adequately resolved in the flow of circulation.[35] With the mediation that results from the struggle between workers and bosses over the setting of wage levels, the two kinds of worker consumption thus tend to complement each

---

See Karl Marx, *Grundrisse,* 420–21. [Original: Karl Marx, "Principes d'une critique de l'économie politique," 267–68.]

34. In fact, as Marx demonstrates, both types of consumption correspond to productive consumption from capital's point of view. Moreover, "the individual consumption of the worker is unproductive even from his own point of view, for it simply reproduces the needy individual; it is productive to the capitalist and to the state, since it is the production of a force which produces wealth for other people." Karl Marx, *Capital,* vol. 1, 719. [Original: Literal translation of Karl Marx, *Le capital, Oeuvres,* vol. 1, ch. 23, 1075; see also *El capital,* vol. 1, ch. 21, 482.]

35. "The individual consumption of the worker and that of the non-accumulated part of the surplus product encompass the totality of individual consumption. This conditions, in its totality, the circulation of capital." Literal translation of Karl Marx, *Le capital, Oeuvres,* Économie 2, 543; see also Marx, *Capital,* vol. 2, 173. [Original: Karl Marx, *Le capital. Oeuvres,* vol. 2, 543; see also *El capital,* vol. 2, 84.]

other in the course of the cycle of capital; in this way, they overcome the initial situation of opposition in which they found themselves. This is, moreover, one of the reasons why the dynamics of the system tend to be channeled through relative surplus value, which ultimately implies a decrease in the price of the commodities comprising the worker's individual consumption.

In the Latin American export economy, things work in a different way. Because circulation is separated from production and takes place basically in the sphere of the external market, the worker's individual consumption does not interfere with the realization of the product, although it does determine the rate of surplus value. As a result, the system's natural tendency will be to exploit the worker's labor power to its very limit, without worrying about creating conditions for him to replenish it, provided that new hands can replace him in the productive process. The tragedy for Latin America's working population is that this assumption was always thoroughly fulfilled: the existence of Indigenous labor reserves (as in Mexico) or of migratory flows derived from the displacement of European labor, spurred by technological progress (as in South America), allowed for a constant increase in the mass of workers up until the beginning of this century. The result has been to give free rein to the shrinking of the worker's individual consumption and, therefore, to the super-exploitation of labor.

The export economy is therefore more than a mere product of an international economy based on productive specialization: it is a social formation based on the capitalist mode of production, which accentuates the contradictions inherent to capitalism to the limit. In doing so, it configures the exploitative relations on which it is based in a specific way, and creates a cycle of capital that tends to reproduce the dependency in which it finds itself vis-à-vis the international economy on an expanded scale.

It is thus that worker's individual consumption is sacrificed for the sake of exports to the world market, depressing levels of domestic demand, and making instead the world market the only outlet for production. At the same time, the increase in profits resulting from this puts the capitalist in a position to develop consumer expectations without any counterpart in domestic production (oriented toward the world market); these expectations must be satisfied through imports. The separation between individual consumption based on wages and individual consumption generated by non-accumulated surplus value thus gives rise to a stratification of the domestic market, which is also a differentiation between spheres of circulation: whereas the "low" sphere in which workers take part—which the system strives to restrict—is based on domestic production, the "high" sphere of circulation, the preserve of non-workers—which the system tends to widen—is linked to external production through imports.

The harmony created, at the level of the world market, between Latin America's exports of raw materials and foodstuffs and its imports of European manufactured consumer goods, conceals the tearing apart of the region's economy, expressed by the fracturing of total individual consumption into two opposing spheres. When the world capitalist system reaches a certain level of development, and Latin America enters the stage of industrialization, the latter will have to do so based on the foundations created by its export economy. The profound contradiction that characterizes that economy's capital cycle and its effects on labor exploitation will have a decisive effect on the course that the Latin American industrial economy takes, which explains many of the problems and tendencies that it currently presents.

## THE PROCESS OF INDUSTRIALIZATION

This is not the place to enter into an analysis of the industrialization process in Latin America, much less to take a position in the current dispute over the role that import substitution played in this process.[36]

---

36. The thesis of import-substitution industrialization was central to the developmentalist ideology, whose great epigone was the United Nations Economic Commission for Latin America (CEPAL). The classic work in this context, María da Conceição Tavares's study of Brazilian industrialization, was originally published as United Nations, "The Growth and Decline of Import Substitution in Brazil," in the *Economic Bulletin for Latin America* 9, no. 1 (March 1964). In recent years, debates focusing on this thesis, though not detracting from its validity,

For the purposes we have proposed, it is enough to note that, however significant industrial development might have been within the export economies (and hence, in the extension of domestic markets) in countries like Argentina, Mexico, Brazil, and others, it never reached the point of forming a true industrial economy, one which, by defining the character and direction of capital accumulation, would have brought about a qualitative change in the economic development of these countries. On the contrary, industry continued to be an activity subordinated to the production and export of primary goods, which in fact constituted the vital center of their accumulation processes.[37] It is only when the crisis of the international capitalist economy—during the period between the First and Second World Wars—hinders accumulation based on production for the external market, that the axis of accumulation shifts toward industry, giving rise to the modern industrial economy that now prevails in the region.

From the perspective that interests us, this means that the upper sphere of circulation, which was articulated with the external supply

have tended to qualify the role played by import substitution in Latin America's industrialization process. A good example is Don L. Huddle's article, "Reflexões sobre a industrialização brasileira: fontes de crescimento e da mudança estrutural, 1947/1963," in the *Revista Brasileira de Economia* 23, no. 2 (1969). On another note, some authors have been more concerned with the situation of industry in the Latin American economy before the acceleration of import substitution; an important work in this line of investigation is Vânia Bambirra's essay, *Hacia una tipología de la dependencia: industrialización y estructura socio-económica* (Santiago: Centro de Estudios Socio-Económicos, Universidad de Chile, 1971).

37. It is interesting to note that industry that complements exports represented the most active sector of the export economy's industrial activities. In this sense, the available data for Argentina show that, in 1895, the capital invested in industry producing for the domestic market represented about 175 million pesos, in contrast to the more than 280 million pesos invested in industry linked to exports. In the former, which clearly consititued an artisanal sector, the average capital per firm was only 10,000 pesos, while it rose to 100,000 pesos in the latter. See Roberto Cortés Conde, "Problemas del crecimiento industrial (1880–1914)," in Torcuato S. Di Tella et al., *Argentina, sociedad de masas* (Buenos Aires: Editorial Universitaria de Buenos Aires, 1965).

of manufactured consumer goods, shifts its center of gravity toward domestic production, its parabola coinciding *grosso modo* with that representing the lower sphere, proper to the working masses. It would appear, then, that the eccentric movement exhibited by the export economy was beginning to correct itself, and that dependent capitalism was moving toward a configuration similar to that of the classical industrial countries. It was on this basis that the various so-called developmentalist currents flourished in the 1950s, which alleged that the economic and social problems afflicting the Latin American social formation were due to its insufficient capitalist development, and that accelerating this development would be enough to make them disappear.

In fact, the apparent similarities between the dependent industrial economy and the classical industrial one concealed profound differences that capitalist development would only heighten, rather than attenuate. The internal reorientation of demand, generated by unaccumulated surplus value, already implied a specific mechanism for the creation of a domestic market that was radically different from the one operating in the classical economy. This in turn would have serious repercussions on the form taken by the dependent industrial economy.

In the classical capitalist economy, the formation of the internal market is the counterpart of the accumulation of capital: by separating the producer from the means of production, capital not only creates the wage earner, that is, the worker who has only his labor power to dispose of, but also creates the consumer. In effect, the worker's means of subsistence, previously produced directly by him, are incorporated into capital as a material component of variable capital, and are only returned to the worker once he purchases their value in the form of a wage.[38] There is therefore a strict correspondence between the pace of accumulation and that of market expansion. The possibility for the industrial capitalist to acquire the foodstuffs necessary for the worker from abroad, at a low price, leads to a tightening of the nexus between

---

38. The expanded reproduction of this relationship constitutes the very essence of capitalist reproduction. See particularly Karl Marx, *Capital*, vol. 1, ch. 26. [Original: Karl Marx, *El capital*, vol. 1, ch. 24.]

accumulation and the market, once the part of the worker's individual consumption devoted to absorbing manufactured products increases. It is for this reason that industrial production in this kind of economy basically centers on popular consumer goods and seeks to make them cheaper, since they have a direct effect on the value of labor power, and therefore—to the extent that the struggle between workers and bosses tends to bring wages closer to that value—on the rate of surplus value. We have already seen that this is the main reason why the classical capitalist economy must be oriented toward increasing labor's productivity.

The development of accumulation based on labor productivity results in the increase of surplus value, and consequently, of the demand created by the part of surplus value that is not accumulated. In other words, the individual consumption of the non-producing classes rises, thus widening the sphere of circulation that corresponds to them. This not only drives the growth of production of manufactured consumer goods in general, but also that of luxury items.[39] Circulation therefore tends to fracture into two spheres, in a manner similar to that seen in the Latin American export economy, but with a substantial difference: the upper sphere's expansion results from transforming the conditions of production, and is made possible to the extent that, as labor productivity increases, the worker's share of total individual consumption decreases in real terms. The existing link between the two spheres of consumption stretches, but does not break.

Another factor helping to prevent this rupture from taking place is the way the world market expands. The additional demand for luxury products created by the external market is necessarily limited because, first, when trade is carried out between nations producing these goods, one nation's advance implies another's retreat, which gives rise to defensive mechanisms on the part of the latter; and because, second, in the case of exchange with dependent countries, this demand is restricted to the upper classes, and so is constrained by the severe income concentration entailed by labor super-exploitation. For the production of

39. Karl Marx, *Capital,* vol. 1, ch. 15, 572–73. [Original: Karl Marx, *El capital,* vol. 1, ch. 13, 370.]

luxury goods to expand, these goods must change their character; that is, they must become items of popular consumption *within the industrial economy itself.* The circumstances that make it possible to raise real wages in this context (something occurring from the second half of the previous century onward, and not unrelated to the devaluing of foodstuffs and the possibility of redistributing internally a part of the surplus extracted from dependent nations) help to counteract the disruptive tendencies at play at the level of circulation, insofar as they expand the individual consumption of workers. Latin American industrialization[40] takes place on different grounds. The permanent pressure exerted by the export economy on the worker's individual consumption only permitted the creation of a weak industry, which would only expand when external factors (such as, in certain conjunctures, trade crises and, for reasons mentioned above, the limiting of trade balance surpluses) partly closed the access of the upper echelon of consumers to imports.[41] It is the greater incidence of these factors, as we have

_____

40. We use the term "industrialization" to refer to the process by which industry, embarking on a qualitative, total overhaul of the old society, marches in the direction of becoming the axis of capital accumulation. It is for this reason that we believe that there is no process of industrialization at the heart of the export economy, even though industrial activities can be observed there.

41. A Brazilian historian, referring to the campaign that Brazilian industrialists initiated in 1928 to raise customs duties, clearly identifies the mechanism by which the industrial sector expanded in the export economy: "Under the pressure of a reduced demand for low quality fabrics in rural areas, as a result of the fall in coffee prices (the average price of a sixty-kilo bag fell from $215 to $170 between 1925 and 1926), various industrialists began to specialize in the production of medium and fine fabrics from the mid-1920s onward. As they penetrated this segment of the market, they began to suffer the impact of English competition, which was accused of *dumping* in order to liquidate domestic production. The industrial centers came together in a campaign aiming to raise tariffs on cotton fabrics and to restrict imports of machinery, claiming that the market could not withstand the expansion of existing productive capacity." Boris Fausto, *A revolução de 1930: historiografia e história,* 16th ed. (São Paulo: Companhia das Letras, 1997), 50. [Original edition: 1970, 33–34, literal translation, italics in the original.] The episode is instructive: the fall in coffee prices restricts not only workers' purchasing power, but also the capacity to import to attend to the high sphere of circulation,

seen, which accelerates industrial growth from a certain moment forward, and provokes a qualitative change in dependent capitalism. Latin American industrialization does not therefore create its own demand, as in the classical economies, but rather is born to meet a preexisting demand, and will be structured according to the market requirements emanating from the advanced countries.

At the beginning of industrialization, the participation of workers in the creation of demand does not therefore play a significant role in Latin America. Operating within the framework of an already existing market structure, whose price level acted as a barrier to popular consumption, industry had no reason to aspire to a different state of affairs. At that time, the volume of demand was greater than supply, so the capitalist was not faced with the problem of having to create a market for his commodities, the situation being rather the reverse. Moreover, even when supply comes into balance with demand—which will occur later on—it will not immediately compel the capitalist to expand the market. Rather, it leads him to exploit the margin between market prices and prices of production; that is, to increase the mass of profit as a function of the unit price of the product. To this end, the industrial capitalist will, on the one hand, force prices to rise by exploiting the *de facto* monopolistic situation created by the crisis in worldwide trade and reinforced by customs barriers. On the other hand, and given that the low technological level makes the price of production fundamentally determined by wages, the industrial capitalist will take advantage of the surplus labor created by the very same export economy and which is aggravated by the crisis it is experiencing (one that forces the export sector to shed its workforce), to put downward pressure on wages. This will allow the export economy to absorb large masses of labor, an absorption that will accelerate the concentration of capital in the industrial sector, exacerbated by the intensification of labor and lengthening of the working day.

---

causing industry to move toward the latter and benefit from the better prices it can obtain there. As we shall see, this tropism in Latin American industry occurs not only in the old export economy.

Starting, then, from the mode of circulation that characterized the export economy, the dependent industrial economy reproduces, in a specific way, the accumulation of capital based on the super-exploitation of the worker. Consequently, it also reproduces the mode of circulation corresponding to this kind of accumulation, albeit in a modified form: it is no longer the dissociation between the production and circulation of commodities in relation to the world market at work, but rather the *separation between the upper and lower spheres of circulation within the economy itself*. This separation, in turn, without being counteracted by the factors operating in the classical capitalist economy, takes on a much more radical character.

Dedicated to the production of goods that do not form part of popular consumption, or which do so very rarely, Latin American industrial production is independent of the workers' wage conditions. This is true in two senses. In the first place, the value of manufactures does not determine the value of labor power, since they are not an essential element of the worker's individual consumption; it will not be the devaluation of manufactures, then, that influences the rate of surplus value. This exempts the industrialist from worrying about increasing labor productivity so as to decrease the value of labor power by lowering the value of each unit of product; it leads him instead to seek to increase surplus value through greater exploitation—intensive and extensive—of the worker, as well as by lowering wages beyond their normal limit. In the second place, the resulting inverse relation between the evolution of the supply of commodities and the purchasing power of workers (that is, the fact that the former grows at the cost of the latter) does not create problems for the capitalist in the sphere of circulation, since, as we have indicated, manufactures are not essential elements of workers' individual consumption.

We said earlier that at a certain point in the process, which varies from country to country,[42] industrial supply coincides broadly with existing demand, constituted by the high sphere of circulation. The need then

---

42. For example, in Argentina and Brazil this happened during the transition from the 1940s to the 1950s, earlier for the former than for the latter.

arises to generalize the consumption of manufactured goods, which, in the classical economy, corresponds to the moment when luxury goods had to be converted into goods for popular consumption. This gives rise to two types of adaptation in the dependent industrial economy: the expansion of consumption by the middle classes, which is generated from non-accumulated surplus value; and the effort to increase labor productivity, a *sine qua non* condition for reducing the cost of commodities.

The second movement would normally tend to provoke a qualitative change in the basis of capital accumulation, allowing the worker's individual consumption to modify its composition and include manufactured goods. If occurring on its own, this would lead to a displacement of the axis of accumulation, from the exploitation of the worker to the increase in the productive capacity of labor. However, it is partially neutralized by the expansion of consumption by the middle-class sectors. This presupposes, in effect, an increase in the income received by these sectors, income which, as we know, is derived from surplus value, and consequently, from the compression of workers' wage levels. The transition from one mode of accumulation to another is therefore difficult and takes place extremely slowly, but it is enough to unleash a mechanism that eventually acts as an impediment to this very transition, while diverting the search for solutions to the realization problems facing the industrial economy.

The mechanism in question is recourse to foreign technology, aimed at raising the productive capacity of labor.

## THE NEW RING OF THE SPIRAL

It is a well-known fact that, as Latin American industrialization progresses, the composition of its imports alters. There is a relative reduction in the level of imported consumer goods, which are gradually replaced by raw materials, semifinished products, and machinery for use in industry. However, the permanent crisis in the external sector of countries in the region does not allow the growing demand for constant capital's material elements to be satisfied exclusively through trade. For this reason, importing foreign capital, in the form of financing and direct investments in industry, becomes particularly important. The ease with which Latin America turns to capital imports abroad is not accidental. It is due to the new configuration assumed by the international capitalist economy in the postwar period. By 1950, the economy had overcome the crisis affecting it since the 1910s and was already reorganized under the aegis of the United States. The degree of concentration of capital that had been achieved on a world scale then places abundant resources in the hands of large imperialist corporations, which they of necessity seek to invest abroad. The significant feature of this period is that this capital flow to the periphery is oriented preferentially toward the industrial sector.

For this reason, while the world economy continued to be in disarray, industrial bases developed in the periphery that offered attractive opportunities for profit-making, thanks to the super-exploitation of labor. But this was not the only, and perhaps not even the most decisive, factor. Over the course of the same period there had been significant developments in the capital goods sector of the central economies. This made it necessary, on the one hand, for the equipment produced there, always more sophisticated, to be applied to the secondary sector of peripheral countries. Thus, an interest in promoting the industrialization process in the periphery arises among the central economies, with the objective of creating markets for their heavy industry. On the other hand, to the extent that the pace of technical progress in the central countries reduced the time needed for replacing fixed capital practically by half,[43] these countries increasingly found it necessary to export equipment and machinery that had become obsolete to the periphery before they fully depreciated.

Latin American industrialization thus corresponds to a new international division of labor. In this framework, the lower stages of industrial production are transferred to the dependent countries (note,

---

43. See Ernest Mandel, *Marxist Economy Theory* (London: Merlin Press, 1974). [Original: Ernest Mandel, *Tratado de economía marxista* (Mexico, D.F.: Ediciones Era, 1969).]

for example, that the steel industry, which was a distinctive marker of the classical industrial economy, has become so widespread that countries like Brazil already export steel), while the most advanced stages are reserved for the imperialist centers (such as the production of computers and the heavy electronics industry more generally, the exploitation of new sources of energy such as nuclear power, etc.), along with a monopoly over the corresponding technology. Going even further, one can discern how the international economy relocates certain rungs not only to the new industrial countries, but also to the older ones so much so that in steel and motor vehicle production, Western Europe and Japan compete advantageously with even the United States, but are not yet able to do so in the machine-tool industry, especially automated machine tools.[44] What we have is a new hierarchization of the world capitalist economy, based on the redefinition of the international division of labor that has taken place over the past fifty years.

Be that as it may, the moment that the dependent industrial economies start looking abroad for technological equipment to accelerate their growth by increasing labor productivity is the same moment that significant capital flows originating in the central countries are directed toward them, flows providing them with the required technology. We will not examine here the effects of the various forms of technological absorption, ranging from donations to direct investment by foreign capital, since this is not very important from the perspective guiding our analysis. We will only concern ourselves with the nature of this technology and its impact on the expansion of the market.

Technological progress is characterized by the saving of the labor power that the worker must devote, whether in terms of time or effort, to produce a certain mass of goods. It is only natural that, overall, this leads to the reduction of productive labor time in relation to the total

---

44. North American production of machine tools doubled between 1960 and 1966, while it grew only by 60% in Western Europe and 70% in Japan. Meanwhile, the manufacture of automated systems developed rapidly in the United States, reaching a value of US$247 million in 1966, in contrast to $43.5 million in Western Europe and only $2.7 million in Japan. Data provided by Ernest Mandel, *Europe versus America? The Contradictions of Imperialism* (London: NLB, 1970), 80n.

time available for production, which, in capitalist society, is expressed as a decrease in the working population, a phenomenon parallel to the growth of the population engaged in non-productive activities, such as services, as well as of the parasitic layers exempt from any participation in the social production of goods and services. This is the specific form that technological development takes in a society based on the exploitation of labor, but not the general form of technological development. It is for this reason that the recommendations that have been made to dependent countries, in which there is much available labor power, that they adopt technologies incorporating more labor power in order to maintain employment levels, represent a double deception: they extol the option of less technological development, and confuse the specifically capitalist social effects of technology with the technology itself.

Moreover, these recommendations overlook the concrete conditions under which technological progress is introduced in dependent countries. Its introduction depends, as indicated, less on those countries' preferences than on the objective dynamics of capital accumulation on a worldwide scale. It was the latter that drove the international division of labor to assume a configuration that opened new channels for the diffusion of technical progress, and which accelerated the pace of this diffusion. The effects of this on the situation of workers in dependent countries could not differ in essence from those inherent to a capitalist society: in other words, the reduction of the productive population and the growth of non-productive social layers. But these effects would have to be modified by the productive conditions that are characteristic of dependent capitalism.

Thus, falling upon a productive structure based on exploiting workers to the utmost, technological progress made it possible for the capitalist to intensify the worker's pace of work, to raise his productivity, while at the same time maintaining the tendency to remunerate him at a rate lower than his real value. To this end, new productive technologies became closely connected to industrial branches that were oriented toward patterns of consumption that, while perhaps transformed into mass consumption in advanced countries, could not be made so under any circumstances in dependent societies. The gulf existing between the workers' standard of living and that of sectors fueling the upper sphere of circulation in such countries makes it inevitable that products such as automobiles, household appliances, and so on, will necessarily be destined for the latter. In this respect, and as long as the goods involved do not enter in workers' consumption, the increase in productivity induced by technology in these productive branches cannot be translated into greater profits by raising the rate of surplus value, but only by increasing the mass of value realized. The spread of technological progress in the dependent economy will thus go hand in hand with greater exploitation of the worker, precisely because *accumulation continues to depend fundamentally more on increasing the mass of value—and hence, of surplus value—than on the rate of surplus value.*

However, by concentrating significantly in branches that produce luxury goods, technological development would end up posing serious problems of realization. The means used to resolve these problems have consisted in state intervention (expanding the bureaucratic apparatus, extending subsidies to producers, and financing luxury consumption), as well as inflation, with the aim of transferring purchasing power from the lower to the higher sphere of circulation; this has entailed lowering real wages even more in order to have sufficient surpluses to carry out income transfers. However, to the extent that workers' capacity to consume is compressed in this way, there is no longer any possibility of stimulating technological investment in the sector of production intended for popular consumption. It should come as no surprise, then, that while luxury goods industries continue growing at elevated rates, those oriented toward mass consumption (the so-called *traditional industries*) tend to stagnate and even decline.

The tendency to bring the two spheres of circulation closer together—something that had been observed from a certain point onward, but which occurred only with difficulty and at an extremely slow pace—could not develop any further. On the contrary, what happens once again is the separation of the two spheres, once the compression of the standard of living of the working masses becomes a necessary condition for expanding the demand created by the strata living off surplus value. *Production based on labor's super-exploitation thus gives rise once again to the mode of circulation that corresponds to it, at the same time as it divorces the productive apparatus from the consumption needs of the masses.* The stratification of the productive apparatus into what have come to be called the *dynamic industries* (branches producing luxury goods and the capital goods mostly used to produce them) and the *traditional industries* reflects how the structure of production adapts to the structure of circulation inherent to dependent capitalism.

But the realignment of the dependent industrial model with that of the export economy does not end there. Acquiring technical progress in conditions of labor super-exploitation brings with it the inevitable restriction of the domestic market, which contrasts with the need to realize ever-increasing masses of value (since accumulation depends more on the mass than on the rate of surplus value). This contradiction could not be resolved by expanding the economy's higher sphere of consumption internally, beyond the limits set by super-exploitation itself. In other words, the dependent industrial economy—unable to extend the creation of demand for luxury goods to workers, and predisposed to the compression of wages that excludes them *de facto* from this kind of consumption—not only had to rely on an immense reserve army, but was also forced to restrict the realization of luxury commodities to capitalists and the upper-middle classes. From a certain moment (which is clearly located in the mid-1960s), the need to expand the cycle of capital abroad arises; that is, to split the cycle of capital—now, however, on the basis of industry—to partially focus circulation *on the world market*. The exporting of manufactured goods (both essential goods and luxury products) has thus become a lifeline for an economy incapable of overcoming the disruptive factors afflicting it. From projects of regional and sub-regional economic integration to the design of aggressive policies of international competition, Latin America is witnessing the resurrection of the old export economic model.

In recent years, the intense expression of these tendencies in Brazil has led us to speak of a "subimperialism."[45] We do not intend to return to the subject here, since subimperialism goes beyond mere economics, and it is not possible to address it without also turning to sociology and politics. We limit ourselves to noting that, in its broadest dimensions, subimperialism is not a specifically Brazilian phenomenon, nor is it an anomaly in the evolution of dependent capitalism. It is true that conditions particular to the Brazilian economy have allowed the country to take its industrialization far, and even to create heavy industry; and that the characteristics of its political society, whose contradictions have given rise to a Prussian-style militaristic state, have led to subimperialism in Brazil. But it is no less true that subimperialism is just one particular form that an industrial economy developing in the context of dependent capitalism can take. In Argentina or El Salvador, in Mexico, Chile or Peru, the dialectics of dependent capitalist development, in its most general features, are not essentially different from what we have sought to analyze here.

To use this line of analysis to study the concrete social formations of Latin America, to orient this study toward defining the root causes of the class struggle unfolding there, and thus, to open up clearer perspectives for the social forces committed to destroying this monstrous formation that is dependent capitalism—such is the theoretical challenge facing Latin American Marxists today. The answer we give will undoubtedly have a considerable influence on the outcome of the political processes that we are currently experiencing.

---

45. My articles on this subject have been brought together in the book, *Subdesarrollo y revolución* [Underdevelopment and Revolution] (Mexico, D.F.: Siglo XXI, 1969). The first of these was originally published under the title, "Brazilian 'Interdependence' and Imperialist Integration," in *Monthly Review* 17, no.7 (December 1965). [TN: *Monthly Review* subsequently published another essay by Marini on the subject of subimperialism. See "Brazilian Subimperialism," in *Monthly Review* 23, no. 9 (February 1972).]

# On the Dialectics of Dependency: A Postscript

Initially, my intention was to write a preface to the preceding essay.[1] However, it is difficult to introduce a work that is itself an introduction. And *The Dialectics of Dependency* does not claim to be anything more than this: an introduction to the theme of inquiry that has been occupying me, and the general lines guiding me in this work. Its publication serves the purpose of putting forth some of the conclusions I have reached—which may perhaps contribute to the efforts of others who are dedicated to studying the laws of development of dependent capitalism—as well as a desire to allow myself to take a comprehensive look at the terrain I am attempting to clear.

I will therefore use this *postscript* to clarify some issues and dispel certain misunderstandings that the text has generated. Indeed, despite the care taken to qualify the most categorical statements, its brevity required painting the trends under study with broad strokes, which at times gave them a very pronounced character. Moreover, the essay's degree of abstraction was not conducive to examining particular situations, which would have allowed a certain degree of relativization to be

1. Translated from Ruy Mauro Marini, "En torno a *Dialéctica de la dependencia*," in *Dialéctica de la dependencia* (Mexico, D.F.: Ediciones Era, 1973), 79–101.

introduced into the study. With no intention of attempting to absolve myself of this, the aforementioned drawbacks are the same as those to which Marx alludes when he warns:

> In theory, we assume that the laws of the capitalist mode of production develop in their pure form. In reality, this is only an approximation; but the approximation is all the more exact, the more the capitalist mode of production is developed and the less it is adulterated by survivals of earlier economic conditions with which it is amalgamated.[2]

That said, the first thing to point out is precisely that the trends outlined in my essay affect different Latin American countries in diverse ways, according to their specific social formations. It is likely that, through faults of my own, the reader may not have noticed one of the assumptions informing my analysis: *the export economy constitutes the transitional stage to an authentic national capitalist economy, which only takes shape when the industrial economy emerges there*;[3] and that survivals of the old modes of production governing the colonial economy still determine, to a considerable degree, the way in which the laws of development of dependent capitalism are manifested in these countries. The importance of the slave-based regime of production in shaping the present-day economy in certain Latin American countries, such as Brazil, is a fact that cannot be ignored.

A second problem concerns the methodology used in the essay, which was made explicit when I pointed to the need to proceed from circulation to production, and to then take on the study of the kind of circulation that this engenders. This method, which has raised some objections, *corresponds exactly to the path followed by Marx*. We need

---

2. Karl Marx, *Capital: A Critique of Political Economy,* vol. 3, trans. David Fernbach (London: Penguin, 1991), 275. [Original source: Karl Marx, *El capital,* vol. 3 (Mexico, D.F.: Fondo de Cultura Económica, 1946–1947), ch. 7, 180. This edition will be cited unless otherwise indicated.]

3. See Jaime Torres's treatment of this issue in "Para un concepto de 'formación social colonial'" (mimeo, Centro de Estudios Socio-Económicos, Universidad de Chile, Santiago, 1972).

only recall how, in *Capital*, the first sections of volume 1 are devoted to issues belonging to the sphere of circulation, whereas the study of production begins only from the third section onward. Likewise, once the examination of general issues has been completed, questions specific to the capitalist mode of production are analyzed in an identical way in the next two volumes. Beyond the merely formal structuring of the exposition, this has to do with the very essence of the dialectical method, which makes the theoretical examination of a problem coincide with its historical development. Thus, this methodological orientation applies not only to the general formula of capital, but also accounts for the transformation of simple commodity production into capitalist commodity production.

This sequence is all the more relevant when the object of study is the dependent economy. Here, we will not dwell on the emphasis given by traditional studies of dependency to the role of the world market (or, to use developmentalist language, the external sector) in generating dependency. Rather, we simply point to one of the central themes of the essay: at the beginning of its development, the dependent economy is entirely subordinated to the dynamics of accumulation in the industrial countries, to such an extent that it is on the basis of the tendency of the rate of profit to fall in these countries (that is, the way in which capital accumulation is expressed there)[4] that the development of dependent countries can be explained. Only when the dependent economy becomes in fact a genuine center of capital production—which entails having its own phase of circulation[5]—and reaches maturity with the

---

4. According to Marx, the tendency of the general rate of profit to fall is nothing other than "*the expression, peculiar to the capitalist mode of production*, of the progressive development of the social productivity of labour," given that "[a]ccumulation itself . . . and the concentration of capital it involves, is simply a material means for increasing productivity." Karl Marx, *Capital,* vol. 3, 319, 324. Emphasis in the original Penguin edition. [Original: Karl Marx, *Le capital. Oeuvres*, vol. 2 (Paris: Nouvelle Revue Française, Gallimard, 1963), 1002 and 1006; see also Karl Marx, *El capital,* vol. 3, 215 and 219.]

5. "Production based on capital originally came out of circulation; we now see that it posits circulation as its own condition, and likewise the production process in

creation of an industrial sector there; only then is there a full manifestation of its laws of development, which always represent a particular expression of the general laws governing the system as a whole. From that moment on, the phenomena of circulation arising in the dependent economy cease to correspond primarily *to problems of realization of the industrial nation to which it is subordinated,* and increasingly become *problems of realization related to its own cycle of capital.*

Moreover, it should also be borne in mind that the emphasis on problems of realization would only be open to criticism if it were done at the expense of examining the conditions in which production takes place, and did not help to explain them. That said, having noted the divorce between production and circulation in the dependent economy (and having stressed the particular forms that this divorce takes during different phases of its development), we insisted a) on the fact that this divorce is generated by the particular conditions that labor exploitation acquires in this economy—conditions that I called super-exploitation; and b) on the way that these conditions permanently bring about, from the very heart of production, factors that aggravate this divorce and lead to serious problems of realization as the industrial economy takes shape.

## TWO MOMENTS IN THE INTERNATIONAL ECONOMY

It is this perspective that allows us to move toward the elaboration of a Marxist theory of dependency. In my essay, I attempted to show that it is as a function of capital accumulation on a world scale (and in particular, as a result of its mainspring, the general rate of profit) that we can understand the formation of the dependent economy. In essence, the steps followed were: a) examining the problem from the perspective of

---

its immediacy as moment of the circulation process, as well as the circulation process as one phase of the production process in its totality." Karl Marx, *Grundrisse: Foundations of the Critique of Political Economy* (Rough Draft), trans. Martin Nicolaus (London: Penguin, 1993), 542–43. [Original: Karl Marx, *Elementos fundamentales para la crítica de la economía política (borrador) 1857–1858,* vol. 2 (Buenos Aires: Siglo XXI, 1972), 34.]

the tendency of the rate of profit to fall in the industrial economies, and b) considering the problem in light of the laws at work in international trade, which give it the character of an unequal exchange. My focus then shifts to the internal dynamics of the dependent economy, pursuing the methodological guidelines mentioned above. Given the work's level of abstraction, I was only interested, when developing the theme of unequal exchange, in the capitalist world market in its mature state (that is, the market once fully subjected to the mechanisms of capital accumulation). However, it is worth noting here how these mechanisms came to exist.

For the economies incorporated into the world market, the variation in the degree of development of their productive forces brings with it significant differences in their respective organic compositions of capital, which point to different forms and degrees of labor exploitation. As the exchange between these economies stabilizes, a commercial price tends to take shape whose term of reference is the value of the commodities produced, over and above its cyclical variations. As a result, the degree of participation in the overall value realized in international circulation is greater for economies with a lower organic composition (in other words, for dependent economies). *In strictly economic terms,* the industrial economies confront this situation by resorting to mechanisms that have the effect of exaggerating the initial differences under which the exchange took place. In this way, they make use of the increase in their productivity to lower their commodities' individual value in relation to the average value that is in effect, and thus increase their share in the total amount of value exchanged; this can be observed both between individual producers within the same nation and between competing nations. However, this procedure, which represents an attempt to circumvent market laws through their very application, entails a rise in the organic composition of capital and activates the declining tendency of the rate of profit, for reasons set out in my essay.

As we saw there, the operation of the industrial economies has an impact on the world market, tending to inflate the demand for food and raw materials. Yet the response of the export economy is the exact opposite: instead of turning to increased productivity, or at least making such a shift a matter of priority, it turns to greater extensive and intensive use of labor power. Consequently, its organic composition falls, and the value of the commodities produced increases, which makes surplus value and profit rise simultaneously. At the level of the market, this causes the terms of trade to improve in its favor, wherever a commercial price has been established for primary products. Hidden behind the cyclical fluctuations of the market, this trend continued until the 1870s. The growth of Latin American exports even led to the appearance of favorable surpluses in the balance-of-trade, which exceeded amortization and interest payments on foreign debt. This, in turn, indicates that the system of credit developed by the industrial countries, which was primarily intended to function as a compensation fund for international transactions, was not sufficient to reverse the trend.

Notwithstanding other factors that act in the same vein (factors relating to the transition from industrial capitalism to the imperialist stage), it is clear that this situation helps to drive exports of capital to the dependent economies, once the profits there become substantial. One of the first consequences of this is a rise in capital's organic composition in these economies and an increase in labor productivity. This leads to a fall in the value of commodities and, in the absence of super-exploitation, should lead to a fall in the rate of profit. As a result, the terms of trade begin to decline steadily, as noted in my essay.

Furthermore, the growing presence of foreign capital in finance, commerce, and even production in dependent economies, as well as in basic services, serves to transfer part of the profits obtained there to the industrial countries. From that point on, the amount of capital relinquished by the dependent economy through financial operations grows more rapidly than the trade balance.

The transfer of profits, and thus of surplus value, to the industrial countries points toward the formation of an average rate of profit at the international level, which frees exchange from its strict dependence on the value of commodities. In other words, the importance that value had in the previous stage as the regulator of international transactions gradually gives way to the primacy of the price of production (the cost of production plus the average profit, which, as we have seen, is lower than surplus value in the case of dependent countries). Only then can it be said that—despite still being hampered by factors of an extra-economic nature, such as colonial monopolies, for example—the international economy reaches its full maturity and brings into play the mechanisms proper to capital accumulation on an increasing scale.[6]

To avoid any misconceptions, let us recall that the fall of the rate of profit in dependent countries, as a counterpart to the increase of their organic composition, is compensated by procedures of labor super-exploitation, in addition to the peculiar circumstances in agricultural and mining economies that foster the high profitability of variable capital. Consequently, the dependent economy continues to increase its exports at prices that are continually more favorable for the industrial countries (with well-known effects on their internal accumulation), while simultaneously maintaining its attractiveness to foreign capitals, which allows the process to continue.

## CAPITALIST DEVELOPMENT AND THE SUPER-EXPLOITATION OF LABOR

It is in this sense that the dependent economy—and therefore, the super-exploitation of labor—appears as a necessary condition of world capitalism, contradicting those who, like Fernando Henrique Cardoso, understand it as something accidental to its development. Cardoso's opinion, expressed in a polemical commentary on my essay,[7] is that, bearing in mind that the specificity of industrial capitalism lies in the

---

6. To quote Marx: "The exchange of commodities at their value, or at approximately these values, thus corresponds to a much lower stage of development than the exchange at prices of production, for which a definite degree of capitalist development is needed." Karl Marx, *Capital,* vol. 3, 277. [Original: Karl Marx, *El capital,* vol. 3, ch. 8, 181.]

7. See Fernando Henrique Cardoso, "Notas sobre el estado actual de los estudios sobre dependencia," *Revista Latinoamericana de Ciencias Sociales* 4 (December 1972): 3–31.

production of relative surplus value, everything related to forms of production based on absolute surplus value, however significant its historical importance, is of no theoretical interest. For Cardoso, however, this does not imply abandoning the study of the dependent economy, once a simultaneous process of development and dependency has begun, which means that, in its contemporary stage, such an economy is also based on relative surplus value and increased productivity.

It should be noted, initially, that the concept of super-exploitation is not identical to that of absolute surplus value, since it also includes a method of producing relative surplus value that corresponds to an increase in the intensity of labor. Moreover, converting part of the wage fund into a fund for capital accumulation does not strictly speaking represent a way of producing absolute surplus value, since it simultaneously affects the two labor times within the working day and not only surplus labor time, as is the case with absolute surplus value. For all these reasons, super-exploitation is defined more precisely by the greater exploitation of the worker's physical strength, as opposed to the exploitation resulting from increasing his productivity, and tends normally to be expressed in the fact that labor power is remunerated below its real value.

This is not, however, the focus of the discussion. What is under discussion is whether forms of exploitation departing from that which generates relative surplus value based on higher productivity should be excluded from the theoretical analysis of the capitalist mode of production. Cardoso's error is to have answered this question affirmatively, as though higher forms of capitalist accumulation *implied the exclusion of lower forms and occurred independently of them*. If Marx had shared this opinion, surely he would not have been concerned with absolute surplus value and would not have integrated it, as a fundamental concept, into his theoretical framework.[8]

---

8. "[T]he production of absolute surplus-value . . . forms the general foundation of the capitalist system, and the starting-point for the production of relative surplus value." Karl Marx, *Capital: A Critique of Political Economy*, vol. 1, trans. Ben Fowkes (London: Penguin, 1990), 645. [Original: Karl Marx, *El capital*, vol. 1, ch. 14, 246.]

Having said that, what my essay intended to demonstrate is, first, that *capitalist production, by developing labor's productive powers, does not eliminate but rather accentuates the greater exploitation of the worker*; and second, that combinations of forms of capitalist exploitation are carried out in an unequal manner in the system as a whole, giving rise to distinct social formations according to the predominance of a given form.

Let us briefly develop these points. The first is key to understanding how the general law of capitalist accumulation works, that is, why there is a growing polarization of wealth and misery at the heart of societies in which it operates. It is from this perspective, and only from this perspective, that studies of so-called social marginality can be incorporated into Marxist dependency theory; in other words, only in this way can the latter theoretically resolve the problem posed by the growth of the very severe forms of relative surplus population that exist in dependent societies, without falling into José Nun's eclecticism, which Cardoso himself so rightly criticized;[9] or into the framework of Aníbal Quijano which, whatever its merits, leads to identifying a marginal pole in these societies in a way that bears no relation to how class contradictions are polarized there.[10] Without claiming to make a thoroughgoing analysis of the problem here, we will set out some explanatory elements based on the above-mentioned theses.

The positive relationship between the increase in the productive capacity of labor and the greater exploitation of the worker, which becomes severe in the dependent economy, is not exclusive to the latter, but rather *is generated by the capitalist mode of production itself*. This is due to the contradictory way that these two fundamental forms

---

9. See José Nun, "Superpoblación relativa, ejercito industrial de reserva y masa marginal," *Revista Latinoamericana de Sociología* 5, no. 2: 178–223; Fernando Henrique Cardoso, "Comentario sobre los conceptos de sobrepoblación relativa y marginalidad," *Revista Latinoamericana de Ciencias Sociales* 24/25 (June–December 1971): 57–76.

10. Aníbal Quijano, *Redefinición de la dependencia y marginalización en América Latina* (mimeo, Centro de Estudios Socio-Económicos, Universidad de Chile, Santiago, 1970).

of exploitation affect the value of what is produced and, therefore, the surplus value that it yields. The development of labor's productive capacity, which implies producing more in the same time and with the same expenditure of labor power, reduces the amount of labor incorporated into an individual product and thus reduces its value, which negatively affects surplus value. More exploitation of the worker is possible via two alternatives: increasing the time of surplus labor (with or without altering the working day); or, without altering the working day and labor times, increasing the intensity of labor. In both cases, the mass of value and the surplus value produced increase, but in the latter (which differs from an increase in productivity because, while more is produced in the same time, it involves a greater expenditure of labor power),[11] once the new degree of intensity becomes generalized, the commodities' individual value decreases and, all things being equal, surplus value likewise diminishes.

In the context of the capitalist regime of production, these opposing tendencies, which derive from the two major forms of exploitation, tend to neutralize one another *once the increase in the productive capacity of labor not only creates the possibility for a greater exploitation of the worker, but leads to that result.* In effect, reducing the total labor time that the worker needs to produce a certain mass of commodities allows capital, *without extending the legal working day or even reducing it*, to demand more effective labor time from the worker, and therefore a greater mass of value. In this way, the threat hanging over the rates of surplus value and profit is fully or partially counteracted. *What appears to be a decrease in working time in the sphere of production becomes, from the point of view of capital, an increase in the production demanded of the worker.*

In the conditions of production, this is reflected in a rise in the organic composition of capital, that is, in the relative or absolute decrease (depending on the pace of accumulation) of variable capital; in other words, in the relative or absolute reduction of the workforce employed and in the expansion of the industrial reserve army.

---

11. Bourgeois economics does not allow this difference to be clearly perceived, since it privileges the product as a term of reference and not labor power.

However, there is a tight interdependence among the growth of productivity, the intensification of labor, and the duration of the working day. Increasing the productive capacity of labor, which implies a lower expenditure of physical strength, is what makes it possible to increase intensity; but this increase clashes with the possibility of extending the working day, and rather works toward reducing it. Conversely, lower productivity limits the possibility of intensifying the pace of work and encourages extending the working day. The fact that, in the highly industrialized countries, the simultaneous increase in productivity and labor intensity has not been translated into a reduction of the working day for several decades does not invalidate what has been said; it merely reveals the working class's inability to defend its legitimate interests, while resulting in the premature exhaustion of labor power, expressed in a gradual reduction of the worker's useful life, as well as in psychophysical disorders brought about by excessive fatigue. In the same vein, the limitations on extending the working day as much as possible that have arisen in dependent countries have forced capital to resort to increasing productivity and the intensity of labor, with predictable effects on the degree to which labor power can be conserved and developed.

What is important to point out here, first of all, is that super-exploitation does not correspond to a survival of primitive modes of capital accumulation, but *is something inherent to the latter that grows in correlation with the development of the productive power of labor.* To assume the opposite amounts to accepting that capitalism, to the degree that it approaches its pure ideal, becomes an increasingly less *exploitative* system, and manages to bring together the conditions for resolving its internal contradictions indefinitely. Secondly, depending on the degree of development of the national economies forming the system, and the development observable in the sectors that comprise each such economy, the greater or lesser occurrence of the forms of exploitation and their specific configuration *qualitatively modify the ways that the system's laws of movement operate,* in particular the general law of capital accumulation. It is for this reason that so-called *social marginality* cannot be treated separately from the way in which, in dependent economies, increases in labor productivity due to the importation of technology intertwine with the greater exploitation of the worker made possible by this growth in productivity.

It is for this reason alone that marginality only reaches its full expression in Latin American countries with the development of the industrial economy.

The fundamental task of Marxist dependency theory is to determine the *specific laws* by which the dependent economy is governed. This presupposes, of course, studying it in the broader context of the laws of development of the system as a whole, and defining the *intermediate steps* through which those laws become specific ones. It is in this way that the simultaneity of dependency and development can be truly understood. The concept of *subimperialism* emerges from the definition of these intermediate steps, and points to the specific operation, in a dependent economy, of the law according to which an increase in labor productivity (and therefore, of the organic composition of capital) leads to an increase in super-exploitation. However, it is clear that this concept does not exhaust the problem in its entirety.

Be that as it may, the requirement that one make the general laws of capitalist development specific precludes, from a rigorously scientific point of view, recourse to generalities, such as the notion that the new form of dependency rests on relative surplus value and an increase of productivity. And it precludes doing so because this is the *general characteristic of all capitalist development*, as we have seen. The problem therefore lies in *determining the character that the production of relative surplus value and the increase in labor productivity assume in the dependent economy.*

In this sense, in my essay, one can find indications—albeit notoriously inadequate ones—that allow a glimpse of the fundamental problem that Marxist dependency theory must confront: the fact that the conditions created by labor's super-exploitation in the dependent capitalist economy tend to hinder its transition from the production of absolute surplus value to that of relative surplus value as the dominant form in relations between capital and labor. The disproportionate weight assumed by extraordinary surplus value in the dependent system is a result of this, and corresponds to an expansion of the industrial reserve army and the strangulation of the capacity to realize production. Far from being mere accidents in the course of dependent development or elements of a transitional order, these phenomena are manifestations of the particular way that the general law of capital accumulation affects the dependent economy. Ultimately, it is once again to labor super-exploitation that we must refer in order to analyze these phenomena.

These are some of the substantive issues raised in my essay that called for greater detail and for clarification. They reaffirm the central thesis sustained therein, that is, that the basis of dependency is the super-exploitation of labor. In this brief note, it remains only to warn that the implications of super-exploitation transcend the level of economic analysis and must also be studied from a sociological and political point of view. It is by moving forward in this direction that we can hasten the birth of the Marxist theory of dependency and free it from the functional-developmentalist characteristics that have accompanied it since its inception.

## REFERENCES

Bairoch, Paul. *Revolución industrial y subdesarrollo* [The Industrial Revolution and Underdevelopment]. Mexico, D.F.: Siglo XXI Editores, 1967.

Bambirra, Vânia. *Hacia una tipología de la dependencia: industrialización y estructura socio-económica* [Toward a Typology of Dependency: Industrialization and Socio-economic Structure]. Santiago: Centro de Estudios Socio-Económicos (CESO), Universidad de Chile, 1971.

Barboza-Carneiro, Julio Augusto. *Situation économique et financière du Brésil: mémorandum présenté à la Conférence Financière Internationale* [The Economic and Financial Situation of Brazil: Memorandum Presented at the International Financial Conference]. Brussels: Société des Nations, 1920.

Canguilhem, Georges. *The Normal and the Pathological.* New York: Zone Books, 1991.

———.*Lo normal y lo patológico.* Buenos Aires: Siglo XXI, 1971.

Cardoso, Fernando Henrique. "Comentario sobre los conceptos de sobrepoblación relativa y marginalidad" [Commentary on the Concepts of Relative Overpopulation and Marginality], *Revista Latinoamericana de Ciencias Sociales* 24/25 (June–December 1971): 57–76.

———. "Notas sobre el estado actual de los estudios sobre dependencia,"

[Notes on the Current State of Studies on Dependence], *Revista Latinoamericana de Ciencias Sociales* 4 (December 1972): 3–31.

Cortés Conde, Roberto. "Problemas del crecimiento industrial (1880–1914)" [Problems of Industrial Growth], in Torcuato S. Di Tella et al., *Argentina, sociedad de masas.* Buenos Aires: Editorial Universitaria de Buenos Aires, 1965.

Fausto, Boris. *A revolução de 1930: historiografia e história, 16ª edição* [The Revolution of 1930: Historiography and History, 16th edition]. São Paulo: Companhia das Letras, 1997.

Frank, Andre Gunder. "Capitalist Underdevelopment or Socialist Revolution." In *Latin America: Underdevelopment or Revolution?*, 371–409. New York: Monthly Review Press, 1969.

———. "Quién es el enemigo inmediato" [Who is the immediate enemy?], *Pensamiento Crítico* 13 (Havana), 1968.

Furtado, Celso. *The Economic Growth of Brazil: A Survey from Colonial to Modern Times*, trans. Ricardo W. de Aguiar and Eric Charles Drysdale. Berkeley: University of California Press, 1963.

———.*Formación económica del Brasil* [The Economic Formation of Brazil], Mexico, D.F.: Fondo de Cultura Económica, 1962.

Halperín Donghi, Tulio. *The Contemporary History of Latin America*, ed. and trans. John Charles Chasteen. London: Macmillan Press, 1993.

———.*História contemporánea de América Latina*. Madrid: Alianza Editorial, 1970.

Huddle, Don L. "Reflexões sobre a industrialização brasileira: fontes de crescimento e da mudança estrutural, 1947/1963" [Reflections on Brazilian Industrialization: Sources of Growth and Structural Change, 1947/1963], *Revista Brasileira de Economia* 23, no.2 (1969): 35–58.

Mandel, Ernest. *Marxist Economic Theory*, trans. Brian Pearce. London: Merlin Press, 1974.

———.*Europe versus America? Contradictions of Imperialism*. London: New Left Books, 1970.

———.*Tratado de economía marxista* [A Treatise on Marxist Economics]. Mexico, D.F.: Ediciones Era, 1969.

Marini, Ruy Mauro. "Brazilian Interdependence and Imperialist Integration," *Monthly Review* 17, no. 7 (December 1965): 10–29.

———. *Subdesarrollo y revolución* [Underdevelopment and Revolution]. Mexico, D.F.: Siglo XXI, 1969.

———. "Brazilian Subimperialism." *Monthly Review* 23, no. 2, 1972.

Marx, Karl. *Oeuvres: Économie 1*, ed. Maximilien Rubel. Paris: Nouvelle Revue Française, Éditions Gallimard, 1963.

———.*Oeuvres: Économie 2*, ed. Maximilien Rubel. Paris: Nouvelle Revue Française, Éditions Gallimard, 1968.

———.*Capital: A Critique of Political Economy*, vol. 1, trans. Ben Fowkes. London: Penguin Books, 1990.

———.*Capital: A Critique of Political Economy*, vol. 3, trans. David Fernbach. London: Penguin Books, 1991.

———.*Capital: A Critique of Political Economy*, vol. 2, trans. David Fernbach. London: Penguin Books, 1992.

———.*El capital*, vols. 1-3. Mexico: Fondo de Cultura Económica, 1946-1947.

———.*El capital*, vol. 1. Buenos Aires: Editorial Signos.

———.*Grundrisse: Foundations of the Critique of Political Economy (Rough Draft)*, trans. with a foreword by Martin Nicolaus. London: Penguin Books, 1993.

———.*Introducción general a la crítica de la economía política, 1857* [General Introduction to the Critique of Political Economy, 1857]. Montevideo: Carabella, n.d.

Marx, Karl, and Friedrich Engels. *The Communist Manifesto*. London: Penguin, 2002.

———.*Elementos fundamentales para la crítica de la economía política (borrador) 1857-1858* [Fundamental Elements for the Critique of Political Economy (Draft) 1857-1858]. Buenos Aires: Siglo XXI, 1972.

———."Manifiesto del Partido Comunista," in *Obras escogidas,* vol. 1. Moscow: Editorial Progreso, 1971.

Nun, José. "Superpoblación relativa, ejercito industrial de reserva y masa marginal" [Relative overpopulation, the industrial reserve army, and the marginal mass]. *Revista Latinoamericana de Sociología* 5, no. 2: 178-236.

Olson, Paul R., and Addison Hickman. *Economía internacional latinoamericana* [Latin American International Economics]. México, D.F.: Fondo de Cultura Económica, 1945.

Quijano, Aníbal. *Redefinición de la dependencia y marginalización en América Latina* (mimeo) [The Redefinition of Dependency and Marginalization in Latin America]. Santiago: Centro de Estudios Socio-Económicos (CESO), Universidad de Chile, 1970.

Santi, Paolo. *Teoría marxista del imperialismo* [The Marxist Theory of Imperialism]. Córdoba, Argentina: Cuadernos de Pasado y Presente, 1969.

Sodré, Nelson Werneck. *Formação histórica do Brasil* [The Historical Formation of Brazil]. São Paulo: Editora Brasiliense, 1968.

Torres, Jaime. "Para un concepto de 'formación social colonial'" (mimeo) [Toward a concept of "colonial social formation"]. Santiago de Chile: Centro de Estudios Socio-Económicos (CESO), 1972.

United Nations [Maria da Conceição Tavares]. "The Growth and Decline of Import Substitution in Brazil." *Economic Bulletin for Latin America* 9, no.1 (March 1964): 1-59.

A young Ruy Mauro (second from the left) with his family.
(Photo courtesy of Felipe Marini and Mathias Seibel Luce)

Marini (right) on Copacabana beach, Rio de Janeiro, soon after entering university, c. 1954. Screenshot taken from the documentary, "Ruy Mauro Marini e a Dialética da Dependência" (Editora Expressão Popular, 2014)

Marini (second from the right) at the Congreso Latino-Americano de Sociología, surrounded by the Guatemalan sociologist Edelberto Torres Rivas (left) and Julio Manduley (right), a Panamanian economist. (Photo courtesy of Mathias Seibel Luce)

Francisco Pineda (left), Ruy Mauro Marini (center), and Jaime Osorio (right) at the latter's home in Mexico City. (Photo courtesy of Jaime Osorio)

(Top and bottom) Photos taken from a series that accompanied an interview with the magazine *Isto É Senhor*, 1987. (Photo courtesy of Mathias Seibel Luce and Agência Isto É)

Ruy Mauro Marini (left), Vânia Bambirra (center), Theotonio dos Santos (far right), and others in Brasília, c. 1985. (Photo courtesy of Mathias Seibel Luce and the Memorial-Arquivo de Vânia Bambirra, Laboratório de Estudos sobre Marx e a Teoria Marxista da Dependência [Lemarx-TMD/ESS], Universidade Federal of Rio de Janeiro and the Núcleo de Pesquisa em História at the Universidade Federal do Rio Grande do Sul)

Marini at the Centro de Estudos Latino-Americanos, UNAM, Mexico City, c. 1995.
(Photo courtesy of Mathias Seibel Luce)

# Dialectics, Super-Exploitation, and Dependency: Notes on *The Dialectics of Dependency*

JAIME OSORIO

1

In the first six decades of the twentieth century, social scientists from diverse fields made many efforts to account for Latin America's particularities.[1] They did so especially between the 1940s and 1960s, when the region became a genuine theoretical problem. The issues of backwardness, which would incorporate those of (under)development, and also questions related to the character of the revolution and its tasks, constituted the axes around which the main proposals and discussions revolved, which soon revealed profound interconnections. Highlighting either the region's semifeudal character, on the one

---

1. This text presented at the commemoration "40 Años de *Dialéctica de la dependencia*" [40 Years of the *Dialectics of Dependency*], Instituto de Investigaciones Económicas, UNAM, Mexico, 2013.

hand, or its capitalist character, on the other, implied not only identifying tactical and strategic tasks in the political terrain, but also offering arguments that were capable of explaining either the backwardness or the capitalist maturity of the region. Similarly, to identify the tasks and projects needed for development or to escape backwardness, such as how to initiate and promote industrialization, implied defining not only the social subjects that should carry out the tasks required (e.g., the industrial bourgeoisie or the state), but also the social classes and sectors that were preventing progress (e.g., oligarchic agrarian groups or mining consortiums).

Economics and politics came together closely in the question of what was to be done to overcome backwardness and underdevelopment, or how to accumulate forces so as to transform the prevailing social order. The Cuban Revolution in the late 1950s unleashed and multiplied these discussions. It forced all social and political forces with projects in play to refine and deepen their positions on the character of the region's economic development and its possible political transformation.

This close link between theoretical/political debates and actual projects of certain social groups (be they classes, fractions, or sectors), and organizations (parties, movements, or academic centers) is key to understanding the richness of the problems raised and the answers reached by Latin American social thought in those years, which was a period without parallel in the history of this tradition.

2

Coming to terms with Latin America as a theoretical and political issue required a profound questioning of the most elaborate formulations from the various schools and trends participating in the debate. For example, those using the Rostownian recipe, dominant in conventional economics, saw the region's backwardness as deriving from a lack of reform and transformation. Were such reforms to be implemented, it would be possible to reach development, by stages, following the model of the industrialized countries!

There was also the model of CEPAL (Economic Commission for Latin America, and later, the Caribbean) based on centers and peripheries, and its proposals regarding industrialization as a means for attaining technological progress. According to this proposal, which needs to be approached critically, the problem of underdevelopment was ultimately the result of trade between nations—caused by the deteriorating terms of trade, to the detriment of the region—a process that could be reversed by industrialization. Importantly, the CEPAL formulation assumed backwardness to stem from an *external process*, the exchange between nations, which implied not questioning the role of the local ruling classes, who were ultimately victims of the centers, from this point of view. Nor did it reveal the forms of capital's reproduction in the region. These issues came to the fore as industrialization advanced in Latin America, and it became clear that that project had not only failed to resolve the problems of backwardness, but that new problems had emerged. These problems included growing poverty in urban centers, early monopolization, and new transfers of resources and profits to the imperial centers—now through the purchase of industrial equipment and technology and as a result of partnerships with foreign capital with investments in the secondary sector.

A significant theoretical leap, connecting what initially appeared to be unconnected, was the later discovery that development and underdevelopment constitute two faces of the same unitary process: the unfolding and expansion of capitalism as a world system. In this view, development is not possible without generating underdevelopment, and underdevelopment is merely the other, necessary result of development. Moreover, dependency, in this view, implies that certain economies are conditioned by the development and expansion of other economies, to which they are subjugated. This reinforces the idea that the world capitalist system constitutes a differentiated unity of diverse forms of capitalism. It is by considering this unity and the differentiated role and location of these different capitalisms that it becomes possible to grasp, and so to explain, the particular dependent capitalism that is now taking shape in Latin America.

### 3

From this perspective, the problem posed requires us to move beyond the fundamentally descriptive notions that underlie, on the one hand, the now dominant categories and concepts and, on the other, current relational concepts, which nevertheless fail to account for the substantive content of those relationships. Instead, one needs an explanatory theoretical framework that reveals the content and consequences of such relations. This implies a radical critique on various levels: of economic history that is preoccupied with highlighting the inexorable succession of modes of production; of sociologism, which uses class struggle to explain everything, without contributing anything to explaining the class struggle itself; of the prevailing economic theory, which takes refuge in models derived from the characteristics and trajectory of the developed world; and of eclectic evasions and orthodoxy understood as repetition. All are trends and tendencies that have prevailed in explanations of the character of Latin American capitalism in different theoretical perspectives.

In this context, it was necessary to re-create Marxism, but not to repeat Marx, because the unprecedented problem was to substantiate the existence of a new modality of capitalism and to define its developmental trends within the framework of this relationship with the capitalist world system. That is what Marini's book, *Dialéctica de la dependencia*, offers to theory and Marxism.[2] No more, and no less.

### 4

The path opened up by *Dialéctica de la dependencia* called into question numerous theoretical positions. As mentioned above, it was not simply a theoretical project, but simultaneously and immediately a political proposal that took a stand on the contemporary relevance of revolution to the region. All felt the blow: classical theorists of development, Cepaline structuralists and developmentalists, organic

_____

2. Ruy Mauro Marini, *Dialéctica de la dependencia* (Mexico, D.F.: Serie Popular Era, 1973).

intellectuals from the local ruling classes, big imperialist capitalists, and orthodox Marxists. Each focused their critique on Marini's thesis, once some of his initial theoretical advances came to light.[3] The criticism only intensified when *Dialéctica de la dependencia* appeared as a book in 1973.

In the seventies and eighties, the counterinsurgent and counterrevolutionary offensive imposed by force on the continent, with the proliferation of military dictatorships and authoritarian civil governments—an assault that would be extended to Europe and the United States, with the accession of the conservative governments of Margaret Thatcher and Ronald Reagan—even reached the region's universities. It led to the marginalization or confinement of Marxism in curricula and programs of study, and to the growing abandonment not only of Marxism's core concepts but also its categories. Hence we no longer speak of *classes*, but rather of *civil society* or *citizens*; no longer of *domination*, but of *governability*; and not of *exploitation*, but of *social inequality* or *poverty*. Along with this long string of defeats, we witnessed the conversion of numerous and important swaths of Marxist intellectuals.

In such a scenario, with so many losses, the abandonment and forcing into oblivion of Marini's theses appeared to be a minor matter. But

---

3. The first part of *Dialéctica de la dependencia* was initially published in *Sociedad y Desarrollo* (1972) with the title "Dialéctica de la dependencia: la economía exportadora." The opening response came from Fernando Henrique Cardoso in a 1972 article for the *Revista Latinoamericana de Ciencias Sociales*. After *Dialéctica de la dependencia*'s publication in 1973, Cardoso and José Serra again critiqued Marini's thesis, now much more aggressively. Marini responded with a substantial piece in *Revista Mexicana de Sociología*. See Ruy Mauro Marini, "Dialéctica de la dependencia: la economía exportadora," *Sociedad y Desarrollo* 1 (January-March 1972): 35–51; Fernando Henrique Cardoso, "Notas sobre el estado actual de los estudios sobre dependencia," *Revista Latinoamericana de Ciencias Sociales* 4 (1972): 3–31; José Serra and Fernando Henrique Cardoso, "Las desventuras de la dialéctica de la dependencia," *Revista Mexicana de Sociología* 40 (Número extraordinario, 1978): 9–55; Ruy Mauro Marini, "Las razones del neodesarrollismo (respuesta a F. H. Cardoso & J. Serra)," *Revista Mexicana de Sociología* 40 (Número extraordinario, 1978): 57–106.

in reality, this contributed to his proposals being excluded from discussion and remaining unknown to successive generations of scholars in the region. A clear case is Brazil, Marini's own country, where his main writings have only begun to see the light of day, in Portuguese, over the last fifteen years. The intellectual and political weight of Fernando Henrique Cardoso, who became president of that country, contributed to this neglect, beyond the factors already noted.[4]

## 5

Marini enumerates and explains a series of processes particular to dependent capitalism, the most notable of which is the rupturing of the cycle of capital; that is, the gap between the spheres of production and realization, whether in foreign markets or in the high sphere of local consumption. These particularities also include a situation in which workers figure as producers but are irrelevant as consumers; the weight of extraordinary surplus value and the difficulty of shifting the process of accumulation to the terrain of relative surplus value; the transfer of value to the imperialist economies through unequal exchange; the severe nature of capital concentration and centralization; and, last but not least, a system of production sustained by super-exploitation.

In *Dialéctica de la dependencia*, Marini deals with each of these features and processes to varying degrees. However, not all have the same weight in the configuration and functioning of dependent capitalism, in spite of their being intertwined and unitary at the level of the whole. Marini clearly establishes a hierarchy, noting that "the basis of dependency is the super-exploitation of labor."[5] He also clarifies that he is referring to "labor power" (not "labor") and that by super-exploitation

---

4. Cardoso's critiques of Marini were widely disseminated in Brazil, contributing to the disregard of Marini's theses and writings. See Fernando Correa Prado, "Otras razones del neodesarrollismo (o porqué se desconoció a la teoría marxista de la dependencia)," *Argumentos* 72 (May–August 2013): 99–126; "História de um não debate: a trajetória da teoria marxista da dependência no Brasil," *Comunicação & Política* 29, no. 2 (2014): 68–93.

5. Marini, *Dialéctica*, 91.

he means the processes of violating the value of *labor power*, whether on a daily basis or in an overall sense. This occurs a few pages later, where Marini specifies that "super-exploitation is defined . . . by the greater exploitation of the worker's physical strength . . . and tends *normally* to be expressed in *the fact that labor power is remunerated below its real value.*"[6]

Marini realized that super-exploitation, as a violation of the value of labor power, was and is a generalized resource available to capitalists throughout the world system, and he reiterated the claim in a 1996 paper.[7] He was aware that the "reduction of wages below the value of labor power," was, according to Marx, one of the mechanisms that capital uses to counteract the fall in the rate of profit.[8] He was also mindful of Marx's countless indications that the mechanism is central to the accumulation process in general. For example, in volume 3 of *Capital*, he writes: "In the chapters on the production of surplus-value it was constantly presupposed that wages are at least equal to *the value of labor-power*. Forcible *reduction* of *wages below this value* plays, however, in practice too important a part.... It, in fact, transforms ... *the laborer's necessary consumption fund* into a *fund for the accumulation of capital.*"[9]

---

6. Emphasis added. Ibid., 92–93. On the development of the concept of super-exploitation, see Jaime Osorio, "Fundamentos de la superexplotación," *Razón y Revolución* 25 (Winter 2013): 9–34.

7. See Ruy Mauro Marini, "Proceso y tendencias de la globalización capitalista," in *La teoría social latinoamericana,* vol. 4: *Cuestiones contemporáneas,* ed. R. M. Marini and M. Millán (Mexico, D.F.: UNAM-Ediciones El Caballito S.A., 1996), 65. Below, I present two ways of contextualizing the preceding quote, while reflecting on the definition of super-exploitation as a general process in the capitalist system.

8. This definition of super-exploitation appears in a footnote in both the Spanish-language edition of *Capital* published by Fondo de Cultura Económica and in the version published by Siglo XXI. In keeping with the German edition, these translations refer to "the reduction of wages below the value of labor power." Karl Marx, *El Capital,* vol. 3 (Mexico, D.F.: Fondo de Cultura Económica, 1973), 235; Karl Marx, *El Capital,* vol. 3 (Mexico, D.F.: Siglo XXI Editores, 1976), 301.

9. Marx, *El Capital,* vol. 3 (FCE), 313.

What, then, does it mean to affirm that super-exploitation is the basis for dependency, if capital resorts to this process throughout the capitalist world system?

Along with generalizing enormous losses of social benefits, the reduction of direct and indirect wages, longer working days and deteriorating working conditions for workers in the so-called central world, and the classic increase in labor's intensity to achieve greater productivity, super-exploitation has also tended to expand during the height of the current world crisis. This is why it has emerged not only in the dependent world, but also in central and imperialist capitalism.

But before making hurried judgments and taking for granted that we are talking about a process with identical attributes both in the center and the periphery, it is worth recalling how in *Dialéctica de la dependencia* Marini maintains that "combinations of forms of capitalist exploitation are carried out in an unequal manner in the system as a whole, giving rise to distinct social formations *according to the predominance of a given form.*"[10]

For this reason, we might therefore ask: Does the undeniable fact that super-exploitation is present both in the center and periphery indicate that it has the same significance in both imperialist and dependent capitalism? Does it mean that it achieves the same predominance, has the same repercussions on the reproduction of capital, and generates the same social formations? If that were so, we would have to clearly say that Marini was wrong to position it as the basis of dependency, and we would have the task of explaining the particularity of what we call dependent capitalism, if indeed the notion has any meaning at all.

The first thing to note is that during a world crisis, such as the present one, capitalism, in any social formation—underdeveloped or developed, dependent or imperialist—resorts to super-exploitation to counteract the falling rate of profit, as Marx himself observed. Furthermore, super-exploitation also occurs in normal periods in the developed world for certain sectors of workers, particularly documented or undocumented migrants, with low wages and long working

---

10. Emphasis added. Marini, *Dialéctica*, 93.

days, who work under relatively more intense conditions than the majority of local workers. The problem is not, therefore, that capital resorts
to super-exploitation in conditions of crisis or among small sections of
workers, or even that it does so by increasing intensity under normal
conditions of reproduction. It is obvious that capital has done so and
will continue to do so. But this—in my opinion—is not the problem.

Those who observe that super-exploitation operates throughout
the system, and then proclaim that it constitutes a generalized process,
thus minimizing or diluting its role in dependent capitalism, make the
following logical extrapolation: if super-exploitation has a *historical
presence* in the totality of the system, then it also has the same *theoretical relevance* throughout the system.

The central issue, as Marini indicates in the quotation above, is to
pinpoint the predominant forms of exploitation in distinct social formations in "normal" periods of reproduction, looking at the sectors
of the working population they affect and *the impact they have on the
reproduction of capital*. This is the central problem: how the predominance of different forms of exploitation and super-exploitation affects
the processes of capital reproduction. That is the key to differentiating
social formations. To analyze super-exploitation in an isolated manner,
as something external to these problems, would surely lead us in the
wrong direction.

6

As we already know, there are three forms of super-exploitation.
One is the appropriation of part of the workers' consumption fund,
which is transferred to the capital accumulation fund; or the payment of a wage lower than the value of labor power, immediately at its
point of purchase-sale. Another is the extension of the working day,
which may lead to the premature exhaustion of workers, from whom
capital appropriates future years of life; since this span of time is not
adequately remunerated, the process affects the total value of labor

power.[11] The third form of super-exploitation involves an increase in productivity, which in turn allows for an increase in the intensity of labor or the reduction of "dead time" during working hours. Capital would prefer every second of the hour to be spent in value production. As in the second case, this third form may lead to the worker's premature exhaustion and the appropriation of future years of work and life, without equivalent compensation or possibilities for recovery. Here, as with the extension of the working day, it is the worker's life fund that is expropriated.

Of these three forms, I maintain that it is capital's *appropriation of part of the worker's consumption fund* that has the greatest impact both for all the processes of super-exploitation that define the reproduction of capital in dependent economies and for the political consequences of the problems mentioned above. Since paying wages below the value of labor power implies the immediate appropriation of an important part of the workers' consumption fund, workers are excluded from participating substantively in the domestic market. In terms of accumulation, workers therefore matter to capital as producers, not as consumers. This fosters the creation of a productive structure that turns its back on the needs of the majority, to the point of spurring the rupture of the cycle of capital, and the creation of patterns of reproduction geared to foreign markets and/or narrow internal markets that require robust purchasing power and thus, concentrated income. In such a setting, the ground for establishing communities is illusory and very fragile. The state is likewise built on weak, fractured foundations, and class struggle comes to be characterized by intense, recurring confrontation. In short, *this form of super-exploitation* is the one that *best connects with the group of processes that define the reproduction of capital and the kind of state that is typical of dependent social formations.*

The appropriation of part of the consumption fund throws children and adolescents prematurely into the job market, and forces workers

---

11. There is a point at which, due to the impossibility of recovering the energy lost, given the level of exhaustion, not even the greatest remuneration can compensate for the increased fatigue.

to accept prolonged working days as a way of obtaining overtime pay. Extending the working day in this way continues to be significant from the standpoint of its effects on the reproduction of capital as a whole in dependent capitalism.

However, the payment of wages below the daily value of labor power, if it becomes socially and historically established, also affects the average wages of a social formation. It *drags down the wages of the rest of the workers*, even though some sectors do not suffer from super-exploitative wages. This, in turn, converts these dependent economies and super-exploitation into "a necessary condition of world capitalism," due to their role and significance in setting the profit rates in the capitalist system as a whole.[12]

With the rise of home-based work and piecework, amid wages that violate value, the intensification of work gathers new impetus in dependent capitalism. Nevertheless, this intensification remains mostly associated with processes of high productivity, accompanied by above-average wages that allow workers to participate in the domestic market in a more significant way. Even with these better wages, the workers experience premature exhaustion, and with that comes the deterioration of living and working conditions, in keeping with the higher rate of intensity.

The expansion of credit offered by companies trading in semi-durable goods (such as televisions, furniture, and refrigerators) allows for expanded consumption by the strata of low-income wage earners. With their extended payment plans, such credit enormously increases the products' real price over the long run, but it also allows workers' purchasing power to be expanded. The process of contracting debt disciplines these sectors, making them more amenable to working for extended hours and intensifying their work. In the case of wage earners with higher purchasing power, social and labor discipline is achieved through the fear of losing their jobs and, with that, the durable goods (homes, automobiles, etc.) they have acquired.

In advanced economies, capitalism may involve elevated productivity

---

12. Marini, *Dialéctica*, 91.

accompanied by intensification, but this does not marginalize its workers from consumption. On the contrary, under normal conditions (in contrast to times of crisis, like the current one) it tends to elevate consumption levels. In periods of crisis, however, reduced wages and prolonged working days, together with increased intensity, will also be present in the core zones.

Based on the pervasiveness of wages that fall below the daily value of labor power, and of the extension of the working day (with intensification playing a lesser role), it can be argued that super-exploitation is the foundation of dependency and *only* of dependent capitalism, inasmuch as it has an impact there on the *forms assumed by the process of reproduction of capital as a whole* and generates specific social formations.

This is not to deny that, in the so-called core countries, the bulk of the immigrant population, many of them undocumented, is subjected to conditions of super-exploitation through the appropriation of consumption funds and the extension of the working day; nor to imply that these workers play an important role in setting the rate of profit in these economies. However, under normal conditions of reproduction, the bulk of the working population in these economies has better working and living conditions, and therefore the situation of the immigrant workers, however grave, *does not define the modalities of capital's reproduction in this context.*

The same can be said of workers in dependent capitalism whose wages and working conditions rise above the prevailing pattern of super-exploitation. It is not their situation that defines the predominant modalities of capital reproduction in such countries. In short, a form of capitalism that under normal conditions mainly super-exploits workers by paying wages below the value of labor power or by prolonging the working day is not the same as another in which the predominant forms of exploitation are the intensifying and prolonging of the working day. The consequences for how capital is reproduced in the two situations are radically different, as are the forms of existence and life of the working population, and the organization of life in common.

7

Another stumbling block for some critics of *Dialéctica de la dependencia* relates to the logic of the so-called law of value and its validity. Their main point can be summarized as follows: the more capitalism expands and advances, so too does the law of value. In this way, value and its mediations—in prices of production and market prices—increasingly become the ground on which market exchanges are generalized. Any process that deviates from this logic, they maintain, is an "anomaly" that sooner or later will tend to be corrected by the law of value's inexorable advance.

To establish another basis for a theory of dependent capitalism, as Marini does by positing a structural and permanent violation of the value of labor power, or the setting of prices of production of commodities above their value (which leads to unequal exchanges at the expense of dependent economies), appears to these critics as an aberration that goes against the very premise of how capitalism develops by extending the law of value.

They assume that one of Marx's historical abstractions—"in the chapters on the production of surplus-value it was constantly presupposed that wages are at least equal to the value of labor-power"—is valid for every historical moment.[13] However, as history develops, the "forcible reduction of wages below this value plays ... in practice too important a part."[14] Thus, in spite of this prior assumption, Marx indicates that "we must stop for a moment to examine" how this supposition is negated in the historical unfolding of capital.[15] This negation is also present in the way the law of value takes effect as it becomes historicized.

Materialist dialectics indicates that every process is made up of some tendencies that affirm it, and others that simultaneously negate

13. This interpretation relies on a special assumption, that wages represent the value of labor power, which Marx makes to explain a particular problem: how surplus value is produced. However, the assumption is not a valid one for Marx's general analysis, and for explaining just any problem.

14. Marx, *El Capital,* vol. 1 (FCE), 505.

15. Karl Marx, *Capital,* vol. 1 (London: Penguin, 1976), 505.

it. Negation is not something alien and external to any process. On the contrary, it is what explains how there is movement at the very heart of what bourgeois science only sees as something still, petrified, and stable.

It is because reality is dialectical and operates through negation that we can affirm that capitalism is simultaneously civilization and barbarity—a proposition that defies formal logic. Negation runs through all great Marxist ideas: the general law of capitalist accumulation indicates that with greater wealth and concentration, capital inevitably produces a higher incidence of poverty and misery in society. The same process of concentration of the means of life and production that gives life to the bourgeoisie also creates the process of dispossession of its own negation, the class of proletariat.

It is precisely because Marini writes about the *dialectics* of the process of dependency (the book's title being more than a rhetorical gesture) that he consistently draws attention to the contradictions and negations that this process generates. For this reason, he argues that with regard to the law of value, "[t]he development of commodity relations lays the foundation for a fuller application of the law of value to take place, but it *simultaneously*," he stresses, "*creates all the conditions* for the *various mechanisms* through which capital *tries to evade*" or negate that law.[16]

8

Regarding exchange between nations, where some produce manufactured goods (or more technologically advanced goods) and others produce raw materials, Marini maintains that the former can evade the law of value, due to "the mere fact" that they "produce goods that the rest do not, or cannot produce as easily ... that is, [they can] *sell their products at prices higher than their value*, thus giving rise to an *unequal exchange*," to the detriment of less technologically advanced nations.[17]

---

16. Emphasis added. Marini, *Dialéctica*, 32–33.
17. Ibid., 34–35.

Additionally, Marini maintains that super-exploitation implies "remunerating" labor power "below its value," which entails violations of the law of value.[18] He writes:

> Called upon to contribute to capital accumulation based on the productive capacity of labor in the central countries, Latin America would have to do so through accumulation based on the super-exploitation of its workers. In this contradiction resides the essence of Latin American dependency.[19]

Further on, Marini maintains that "the dependent economy—and therefore, the super-exploitation of labor [that is, the violation of value]—appears as a necessary condition of world capitalism" and not a purely accidental feature foreign to the laws governing world capitalism.[20] Finally, in this brief outline, let us highlight the role of negation in *Dialéctica de la dependencia,* whereby "super-exploitation does not correspond to a survival of primitive modes of capital accumulation, but *is something inherent to the latter that grows in correlation with the development of the productive power of labor,*" and thus expands with the advance of capital accumulation; super-exploitation is not an early feature, compatible only with the primary stages of accumulation.[21]

The quotations above suffice to illustrate that Marxist dialectics have nothing to do with processes where only the positive exists without its negation, and therefore without contradictions. In the case at hand, capitalism advances by extending the law of value, while simultaneously fostering mechanisms that violate and negate it. Hence, capitalism produces development but also dependency; it produces knowledge and technology, but also intensification of labor and super-exploitation. These are simultaneously modern and contemporary processes but also contradictory ones.

---

18. Ibid., 42.
19. Ibid., 49.
20. Ibid., 91.
21. Ibid., 98.

**9**

Fernando Henrique Cardoso argued that industrial capitalism is based on the production of relative surplus value. This suggests that previous forms of exploitation (for example, absolute surplus value) may have *historical relevance*, but nevertheless lack *theoretical relevance*. With this claim, Cardoso attempted to disqualify super-exploitation as the foundation of dependent capitalism, by suggesting that it is theoretically irrelevant. In his postscript to *Dialéctica*, Marini responds by pointing out that if this were the case, Marx would not have concerned himself with the study of absolute surplus value. More important, he would not have "integrated it, as a fundamental concept, into his theoretical framework."[22]

Marini adds that the real issue for Cardoso's approach is "whether forms of exploitation departing from that which generates relative surplus value . . . should be excluded from the theoretical analysis of the capitalist mode of production." He points out that "Cardoso's error is to have answered this question affirmatively," given that "higher forms of capitalist accumulation" neither exclude *nor occur independently of the lower forms.*[23]

The idea behind Marini's remark is that the emergence of relative surplus value as an advanced form in the development of capitalism does not imply the elimination—either theoretically or historically—of different forms of exploitation. On the contrary, the persistence and expansion of these other forms of exploitation goes hand in hand with the spread of the advanced forms.

As noted above, Marini indicates elsewhere in his writings that "super-exploitation does *not* correspond to a survival of primitive modes of capital accumulation but *is something inherent to the latter that grows in correlation with the development of the productive power of labor.*"[24]

Similar conclusions apply to authors who assume that the advance

---

22. Ibid., 93.
23. Ibid. This error is repeated by the "positive" interpreters of the law of value—those who do not recognize the role of negation.
24. Ibid., 98.

of the law of value implies exchanges around prices of production and market prices, without any transfer of value taking place, much less unequal exchange.[25] On this issue, they position themselves just as Cardoso does: *there are processes that have historical importance, but nonetheless have no theoretical significance.* Thus, it does not matter that the labor of enslaved people has been revived in the capitalism of the twenty-first century, that big capital colludes to fix prices on certain goods, or that shortages of goods are created to raise their prices. Yet these and other processes—where the law of value is called into question—have historical importance, and for this reason one must come to terms with their theoretical significance.

## 10

From time to time, as part of a ritual similar to those carried out in ancient cultures to placate some vengeful god or exorcise an evil spirit, we hear claims that new economies have broken with backwardness and underdevelopment, and are moving toward the goals and blessings of the so-called developed regions and economies. First, it was South Korea, then Malaysia and Singapore; today it is China and perhaps also India. The first surprising thing to note is all the noise generated by conventional economists regarding these scenarios: if they assume that capitalism is a productive organization that leads to development, why all the commotion?

---

25. Juan Íñigo Carrera maintains this thesis. Following Grossmann and Bettelheim, we argue that the conversion of value into prices of production, as the world market reaches maturity, leads to transfers of value from less to more productive capitals. Hence, when we turn to consider trade in the world market, the law of value is reaffirmed, but so too is its negation. Juan Íñigo Carrera, *La renta de la tierra: Formas, fuentes y apropiación* (Buenos Aires: Imago Mundi, 2017); Henryk Grossmann, *La ley de la acumulación y del derrumbe del sistema capitalista* (Mexico, D.F.: Siglo XXI Editores, 1979); Charles Bettelheim, "Intercambio internacional y desarrollo regional," in *Imperialismo y comercio internacional: El intercambio desigual,* ed. S. Amin et al. (Mexico, D.F.: Pasado y Presente, 1981), 33–61.

Some clarifications are warranted about these periodically repeated rituals. At a general theoretical level, Marxist dependency theory indicates that at the heart of the capitalist world system, development in one region or economy requires the extension or intensification of underdevelopment in that region or in other economies in the world system. That is because *one of the central components* of what is called development is the concentration, in some region or economy, of labor and particularly the wealth produced by peoples and economies that are expropriated through the very rules governing international economic relations. This expropriation is achieved through simple plunder (in the setting of colonial relations) or unequal exchange (prices set by those with technological or other advantages). The whole process goes hand in hand with the increased exploitation of the working populations and technological transformations in those economies moving toward development.

Under the logic of value, there is no way to avoid this situation. If China or India are now undergoing processes of development, as many suggest, we could ask from where and how these economies obtain the value that opens the doors to development, and therefore, whose work is fueling the advance of these economies, beyond the worsening of all mechanisms of exploitation among their own working populations.[26]

Turning to more concrete situations, Marxist dependency theory shows that since Latin America became a formally independent region, it has not generated an autonomous, strong bourgeoisie with a political commitment that makes it able to lead processes of development. Under these conditions, faced with a local and regional bourgeoisie that is subjugated to projects of other (usually imperialist) capitals—a bourgeoisie without autonomy, political will, or plans of its own—the underdevelopment that emerged only yielded projects or patterns of reproduction marked by the "development of underdevelopment," as Andre Gunder Frank's apt formulation holds, along with new and more acute forms of dependency.

---

26. See also Jaime Osorio, "Corea del Sur y China: ¿modelos para América Latina?," in *Teória marxista de la dependencia: Historia, fundamentos, debates y contribuciones* (Mexico, D.F.: Universidad Autónoma Metropolitana (UAM)-Xochimilco, 2016), 357–80.

## 11

It is not Marxist dependency theory that rendered the Latin American bourgeoisie incapable of leading development projects. What that theory did is to highlight their incapacity, explaining the reasons for their social and political conduct. Its analysis has shown the naïveté and fallacies of international bodies and academic groups that make extensive descriptive studies and then conclude—like children writing letters to Santa Claus—that it would be good to have a bourgeoisie that is dynamic, autonomous, committed to technological knowledge and development and to establishing knowledge-based societies—a bourgeoisie willing to create internal markets by paying better wages to most of the working population.

Such calls are based on the assumption that the Latin American bourgeoisie could behave differently from the way it actually does. However, these studies leave off precisely where they should begin: by explaining what it is about Latin American capitalist development and the dependent condition that leads to the emergence of the ruling classes that we actually have, and not to those that some would like to have, and which they blissfully suppose emerged in other regions.

## 12

In this context, Marxist dependency theory calls into question the celebratory and superficial accounts claiming that Latin America is currently witnessing neo-developmentalist forces and projects, thanks to the Argentinian, Brazilian, Chilean, and Mexican bourgeoisies. One should recall that the notion of "developmentalism" emerged during the middle of the twentieth century, under the aegis of an industrial bourgeoisie that aspired to pull the region out of backwardness, to close gaps, and to ensure the bulk of the population's welfare. In the end, that bourgeoisie aspired to lead a development project. It is not necessary to review what happened in that historical period. Suffice to say that, as we enter the third decade of the twenty-first century, Latin America as a whole, and each economy with its own particularities, is experiencing situations where merely reaching the wage levels of the 1960s is thought to be an enormous victory. This is occurring after four decades during which the vast majority of the population's standard of living seriously declined, when social inequality reached unprecedented levels, and when poverty and misery affected millions of households, despite the triumphs being touted every so often in the war against poverty.

## 13

This points to how *Dialéctica de la dependencia*'s powerful claims not only resonate with the region's history but also remain enormously relevant today. The launching of a new pattern of capital reproduction—the export model of productive specialization that was forged over the last forty years—has revealed serious imbalances, vulnerability, and degrees of dependency in the region. Building this new export economy was carried out by exacerbating multiple forms of dispossession and exploitation, to make the region's economies competitive in external markets. The very fact that it is an *export* model highlights the primacy of external markets as the locus of realization, at the expense of internal consumption and the domestic market comprising the bulk of the working population. Thus, not just any export economy has been created, but rather one that turns its back on direct producers, thereby opening more room to transfer part of the workers' consumption fund to accumulation funds, while prolonging the working day. All of this aggravates the structural super-exploitation in the region. It is thus not coincidental that the growth and dynamism of regional exports has been accompanied by the collapse of wages and the increasing precarity of jobs, as well as an increase in unemployment and underemployment over the last three or four decades. Unemployment has been weakly curbed in some cases, but in the case of wages, they are always below the levels of the 1960s and 1970s. As such, the most dynamic branches of production have little or nothing to do with the needs of the vast majority of the population.

The unequal distribution of income and the acute concentration of wealth—with 5 or 10 percent of the population appropriating 40 percent or more of the wealth generated—shows how a narrow but powerful domestic market, for those with high purchasing capacity, has been created. This high-level market satisfies its demand for luxury goods through imports or through the local production and assembly (sometimes in maquilas) of products such as iPads, cell phones, televisions, and cars, all leading to the formation of a reduced and narrow bubble of modernity amid generalized barbarity and lives subjected to indignity.

## 14

If economic theses fail to break with those perspectives that, for all intents and purposes, condone the barbarity that the logic of capital imposes on the dependent world, then political theses will not offer correct solutions in the sphere of politics either. Only the end of dominant power relations can open a horizon for a dignified life for the majority of peoples of the region.

## 15

If we leave aside Marini's postscript—*En torno a Dialéctica de la dependencia*, written for its first edition—then *Dialéctica de la dependencia* consists of just 64 pages (each with approximately 50 keystrokes in every one of its 29 lines). In those few pages, characterized by an impressively synthetic language, are the most important explanations offered for Latin American dependency and its main tendencies to date. Arduous years of study and militancy are condensed in these few sheets, which are laden with the future.

# REFERENCES

Bettelheim, Charles, "Intercambio internacional y desarrollo regio-
  nal [International Exchange and Regional Development]," in
  *Imperialismo y comercio international: El intercambio desigual,* ed. S.
  Amin et al., *Cuadernos de Pasado y Presente* 24 (1971).
Cardoso, Fernando Henrique, "Notas sobre el estado actual de los estudios
  sobre dependencia [Notes on the Current State of Studies on
  Dependence]," *Revista Latinoamericana de Ciencias Sociales* 4
  (1972): 3–31.
Correa Prado, Fernando, "Otras razones del neodesarrollismo (o porqué se
  desconoció a la teoría marxista de la dependencia) [Other Reasons
  for Neo-Developmentalism (or why the Marxist theory of dependency
  was ignored]," *Argumentos* 72 (May -August 2013): 99–126.
———. "História de um não debate: a trajetória da teoria marxista da dependência
  no Brasil [The History of a Non-Debate: the trajectory of the Marxist
  theory of dependency in Brazil]," *Comunicação & Política* 29, no. 2
  (2014): 68–94.
Grossmann, Henryk, *La ley de la acumulación y del derrumbe del sistema capi-
  talista* [The Law of Accumulation and the Collapse of the Capitalist
  System]. Mexico, D.F.: Siglo XXI Editores, 1979.
Íñigo Carrera, Juan, *La renta de la tierra: Formas, fuentes y apropriación* [Land
  Rent: Forms, Sources, and Appropriation]. Buenos Aires: Imago
  Mundi, 2017.
Marini, Ruy Mauro, "Dialéctica de la dependencia: la economía exportadora
  [The Dialectics of Dependency: the export economy]," *Sociedad y
  Desarrollo* 1 (enero–marzo 1972): 35–51, https://marini-escritos.
  unam.mx/wp-content/uploads/1991/01/3.3-Diale%CC%81cti-
  ca-de-la-dependencia.pdf.
———. *Dialéctica de la dependencia* [The Dialectics of Dependency]. Mexico,
  D.F.: Serie Popular Era, 1973.
———. "Las razones del neodesarrollismo (respuesta a F. H. Cardoso & J. Serra)
  [The Arguments for Neodevelopmentalism (a response to F. H.
  Cardoso & J. Serra)]," *Revista Mexicana de Sociología* 40 (Número
  extraordinario, 1978): 57–106.
———. "Proceso y tendencias de la globalización capitalista [Process and Trends
  in Capitalist Globalization]," in *La teoría social latinoamericana,*
  vol.4: *Cuestiones contemporáneas,* ed. R. M. Marini and M. Millán.
  Mexico, D.F.: UNAM-Ediciones El Caballito S.A., 1996.
Marx, Karl, *El Capital,* vol. 3. Mexico, D.F.: Fondo de Cultura Económica, 1973.
———. *El Capital,* vol. 3, vol. 6. Mexico, D.F.: Siglo XXI Editores, 1976.
———. *Capital,* vol. 1. London: Penguin, 1976.
Osorio, Jaime, "Fundamentos de la superexplotación [Foundations of
  Superexploitation]," *Razón y Revolución* 25 (second semester, 2013).

———."Corea del Sur y China: ¿modelos para América Latina? [South Korea and China: models for Latin America?]," in *Teória marxista de la dependencia: Historia, fundamentos, debates y contribuciones*. Mexico, D.F.: Universidad Autónoma Metropolitana (UAM)-Xochimilco, 2016.

Serra, José, and Fernando Henrique Cardoso, "Las desventuras de la dialéctica de la dependencia [The Misadventures of the Dialectics of Dependency]," *Revista Mexicana de Sociología* 40 (Número extraordinario, 1978): 9–55.

# Index

servitude, 132

slavery, 12–13, 63n150, 185; in
  super-exploitation, 131, 131n23,
  132–35, 132n26, 133n27; see
  also *Brazil, abolition; servitude*

social class, 80, 86–89, 170, 182,
  187; see also *working class*

social democracy, 88, 94, 96, 99

social marginality, 73, 73n190, 162,
  164–65

socially necessary labor time, 71,
  122; see also *surplus labor time*

Spain, 10, 14–15

state, 74n192, 151, 170, 178;
  bourgeois hegemony in, 87;
  consumption by, 47, 76n203;
  "military fascism" related to,
  86–87, 89; redemocratization,
  88; social democracy in, 88; state
  terror, 47; "state of four powers,"
  89; see also *subimperialism*

structural dualism, 31n29, 37, 42,
  64n154

structuralism, 31–32, 31n29, 47,
  171; see also *specific topics*

student movements, 40–41, 51

*Subdesarrollo y Revolución:* see
  *Underdevelopment and Revolution*

subimperialism, 48n95, 165;
  "antagonistic cooperation" in,
  45–46, 46n81; definition of,
  41–42, 44, 45–46, 47; doctrine
  of continental integration ("loyal
  bargain"), 44; in *Dialectics of
  Dependency*, 152–53, 152n45;
  in *Dialectics of Dependency*
  postscript, 165; in the Dominican

Republic, 45; Marini-Cardoso
  debate and, 67–68, 74n192; in
  *Monthly Review,* 44–45, 44n76;
  study of, 165; super-exploitation
  related to, 47; working class
  in, 46–47; see also *Brazilian
  dictatorship*

super-exploitation, 17, 148, 152;
  capital reproduction and, 19–20;
  capitalism in, 130, 133–34, 135–
  36, 135n30, 136n31, 139, 179;
  in combination with absolute and
  relative surplus value, 64, 132;
  definition of, 17, 63–64, 72, 130,
  157, 161, 175nn7–8, 177–78; in
  *Dialectics, Super-Exploitation,
  and Dependency,* 174–78,
  175nn7–8, 178n11, 179, 180,
  183; in *Dialectics of Dependency*,
  130–32, 133–35, 137, 139,
  143–46, 148, 152; in *Dialectics of
  Dependency postscript*, 157, 159,
  160–66; appropriation of workers'
  consumption fund, 18, 64, 130,
  142, 161, 175, 177; premature
  exhaustion of labor power, 12, 72,
  132, 134, 164, 177, 178; labor
  times and, 130, 133–34; wage
  labor and, 133; wages below the
  value of labor power, 17, 132,
  161, 175; see also *specific topics*

surplus labor time, 64, 72, 122,
  130, 161, 163; see also *socially
  necessary labor time; surplus
  value, absolute*

surplus value, 98, 139, 161, 161n8,
  163, 163n11, 181, 184; absolute

181; evasion of, 127–28;
globalization of, 98; in *Dialectics
of Dependency,* 127, 128; in
*Dialectics, Super-exploitation,
and Dependency,* 181–83,
184n23, 185, 185n25
value transfer, 62, 128; and
monopolies, 128, 145
Vargas, Getúlio, 42

Weeks, John, 76n203
working class, 25, 35–36; definition
of, 97–98; in England, 64–65;
global, 25; in integration into
world market, 119–20, 120n14; in
subimperialism, 46–47

world economy, 64n154, 65–66,
185n25; see also *international
economy*
world market: foodstuffs in, 119–20,
119n13, 123, 123n17, 124, 125;
integration of Latin America into,
116–21; international division of
labor and, 16, 25, 117, 118, 120,
123, 127, 148–49; raw materials
in, 123–24, 125n19, 128–29,
129n21; manufactures in, 62,
116, 125n19, 128, 146

"Yo pisaré las calles nuevamente"
(Milanes)

**RUY MAURO MARINI** (1932–1997) was one of the originators of Marxist dependency theory. As a result of his activism, the Brazilian sociologist and revolutionary was forced into two decades of bitter exile in Chile and Mexico — and in the process introduced such concepts as "superexploitation," "subimperialism" to the revolutionary lexicon. After receiving amnesty in the early 1980s, Marini returned to his country of birth, dying in Rio de Janeiro in 1997.

**AMANDA LATIMER** is a senior lecturer in Politics & International Relations at Kingston University, UK. Her research examines workers' opposition to the neoliberal crisis of work and free trade agreements in Brazil.

**JAIME OSORIO** is a Chilean social scientist and former colleague of Marini who has resided in Mexico since the military coup of Augusto Pinochet and continued to develop the Marxist theory of dependency ever since.